LIFE OF THE TANAGER

Spangle-cheeked Tanager *Tangara dowii*
Sexes alike. Costa Rica and western Panama.

Sooty-capped Bush-Tanager *Chlorospingus pileatus*
Sexes alike. Costa Rica and western Panama.

Common Bush-Tanager *Chlorospingus ophthalmicus*
Sexes alike. Central Mexico to northwestern Argentina.

Life of
the Tanager

BY

Alexander F. Skutch

ILLUSTRATED BY

Dana Gardner

COMSTOCK PUBLISHING ASSOCIATES a division of

CORNELL UNIVERSITY PRESS | Ithaca and London

First published 1989 by Cornell University Press.

Library of Congress Cataloging-in-Publication Data

Skutch, Alexander Frank, 1904–
    Life of the tanager.

    Bibliography: p.
    Includes index.
    1. Tanagers. I. Gardner, Dana. II. Title.
QL696.P282S58   1989   598.8'82   88-47765
ISBN 0-8014-2226-4 (alk. paper)

Printed in the United States of America.
Color plates printed in Hong Kong.

To Dodge and Lorna Engleman,
who have helped many people
to know tanagers and other birds

Contents

Illustrations and Tables

Color plates

Figures

Tables

Preface

The beauty of tanagers has led many people to photograph or paint them. For many species it is much easier to find color pictures than information about how they live, in part because it is so difficult to locate their nests in lowland tropical forests or on steep Andean slopes. Perhaps, too, these rather typical passerine songbirds seem less likely to invite prolonged study than such divergent birds as hummingbirds, woodpeckers, and manakins. Such neglect of tanagers is lamentable, for this family of about 230 species reveals a fascinating diversity of habits as well as habitats. Not only are tanagers principal contributors to the beauty of tropical American bird life; they are also important distributors of the seeds of tropical trees, shrubs, and vines and hence are of great ecological significance.

When I wrote *The Life of the Hummingbird* and *Life of the Woodpecker*, I could draw on an extensive literature as well as on my own studies of the living birds. Since fewer people have studied and written about the lives of tanagers, in preparing this book I have had to depend largely on my own observations, gathered over more than fifty years. I tell of unusual things I have seen them do as well as of the regularities in their lives. I have endeavored to present tanagers as living birds that eat, sleep, sing, nest, and try to avoid their enemies. Dana Gardner has portrayed them as birds of great beauty.

I have omitted from this book the Swallow-Tanager of tropical South America and eastern Panama. Although sometimes classified as a subfamily or tribe of the tanagers, this species differs greatly from tanagers in its wings, bill, and habits. It therefore seems better to follow the long-established classification that places it in a separate family, the Tersinidae.

To avoid the repetition of scientific names from chapter to

chapter and to provide a ready reference, I give in the index the Latin names of all organisms; vernacular names are used in the text whenever possible. For those who wish to know the published sources of the information contained in the book, or who want to learn about the lives of tanagers in greater depth, the bibliography gives full citations of the books and papers I consulted.

Both artist and author thank the Western Foundation of Vertebrate Zoology, the Los Angeles County Museum of Natural History, and the Universidad de Costa Rica for generously lending specimens that helped to illustrate this book.

ALEXANDER F. SKUTCH

"Los Cusingos,"
San Isidro de El General, Costa Rica

LIFE OF THE TANAGER

1 The Tanager Family

To stand in bright morning sunshine before a tree laden with ripening berries is one of the great delights of bird-watching in tropical America. Among the constantly changing throng of birds that gather for the feast are brisk, tiny manakins, flycatchers large and small, plainly clad thrushes and vireos, woodwarblers, and woodpeckers. But nearly always the tanager family provides the greatest number of species and individuals, and most of the color. Of the forty-four species, from chachalacas and pigeons to sparrows and seedeaters, which, around our house in Costa Rica, eat the sweetish, juicy, deep purplish berries of *Miconia trinervia*, a small tree of the melastome family, fifteen are tanagers. What a brilliant assemblage they are, displaying the whole spectrum of colors from red to violet! The fascinated eye cannot rest as these so varied visitors, each in its own way, while perching, or clinging, or in flight, pluck berry after berry, rarely interfering with other birds. To contemplate the harmony that prevails in this gathering of frugivorous birds increases the pleasure of watching them. They never try to drive other birds away from food, as hummingbirds in the Americas and honeyeaters in Australia frequently do.

Although with patience one can count more than a dozen kinds of tanagers at a single fruiting tree, they are only a small representation of the 230 species in this great family of arboreal songbirds, the Thraupidae, confined to the continents and islands of the Western Hemisphere, chiefly in the tropics. Ranging in length from about 3.5 to, rarely, 11 inches (9–28 cm), clad in the most varied colors in the most diverse patterns, tanagers contribute more than any other family to the splendor of tropical American birds. Hummingbirds, which are possible rivals in splendor, are more numerous in species and perhaps in individuals; but they are smaller and move more swiftly, and their glittering metallic colors glow in full refulgence only when they are viewed from certain angles.

Tanagers are so closely related to buntings, cardinals, grosbeaks, and other emberizine finches that they are sometimes classified as a subfamily, the Thraupinae, of the Emberizidae. However, they prefer fruits to the seeds that figure so largely in the diet of finches. The bills of tanagers vary from short and stout to long and slender, often with a tiny hook at the end of the upper mandible and a somewhat prominent notch behind the tip. Like related buntings, wood-warblers, and icterids, their wings have only nine functional primary feathers, instead of the more usual ten in passerine birds. Despite resemblances, a certain indefinable quality that grows with familiarity enables the bird-watcher to distinguish most tanagers from finches as they flit among the trees.

Although some tanagers inhabit arid scrub, most prefer more humid regions, where they frequent both forests and clearings, including plantations, gardens, parks, and tangled second growth. In the tropics, where they abound, they thrive from warm lowlands to frosty heights. Like other frugivorous birds, they wander rather widely, as trees, now here, now there, ripen their fruits. Some move up and down the mountains with the changing seasons, but those that nest within the tropics are not known to undertake long migrations.

The chief migrants in the family are the four species that breed north of Mexico. The greatest traveler is the Scarlet Tanager, which, after nesting in the woodlands of southeastern Canada and of the eastern United States, winters in northwestern South America, from Colombia to Bolivia. With a single known exception, the Scarlet is the only tanager that exhibits pronounced seasonal changes in coloration—the brilliant scarlet-and-black males becoming greenish and yellow, much like the females, during the winter months. Summer Tanagers breed farther south in the United States and winter from Mexico to Bolivia; the adult male retains the same bright red plumage at all seasons. The male of the Western Tanager, which nests on the Pacific side of temperate and subarctic North America and migrates no farther than Costa Rica, becomes somewhat duller in winter. The northern race of the Hepatic Tanager, which breeds from the southwestern United States to Nicaragua and winters in the southern part of its breeding range, keeps the same colors throughout the year, as do the southern races of this very widespread species.

South American birds tend to be less migratory than North American birds. Three species of tanagers that nest as far south as central Argentina—the Diademed Tanager, Sayaca Tanager, and Blue-and-yellow Tanager—arrive there in the austral spring, rear their young, then withdraw to tropical South America, where they are widely distributed, showing the same colors at all seasons.

The forty-seven species of the largest genus, *Tangara*, often called callistes, display such a vast diversity of colors in such varied patterns that it is difficult to choose one that surpasses all the others in beauty; but certainly none is more richly colored than the Paradise Tanager, one race of which has a plumage of shining apple green, golden yellow, scarlet, bright turquoise, purplish blue, and velvety black. In small flocks, these lovely birds wander through the forests of northern South America from eastern Colombia to Bolivia, the Guianas, and Amazonian Brazil. The sexes are alike, as in many species of *Tangara*, and the colors stay the same throughout the year.

In other genera, the sexes may be equally brilliant or equally plain. Among the bush-tanagers, *Chlorospingus*, which are prevalent in highland woods from Mexico to northern Argentina, both sexes are a plain olive green. Other tanagers of high mountain areas are no less elegant than those of lower and warmer regions. Among them are the splendid mountain-tanagers of the genera *Anisognathus* and *Buthraupis*, which are black or blue adorned with red or yellow; the glittering green Orange-eared Tanager of the genus *Chlorochrysa*; and the Grass-green Tanager of the genus *Chloronis*. Males of *Ramphocelus*, black with scarlet, crimson, or yellow, have much less vivid mates. In the genus *Tachyphonus*, males are largely black, with patches of white, yellow, or red; females are brown, olive, or pale yellow. Quite different from other members of the family is the largest, the

Blue-winged Mountain-Tanager *Anisognathus flavinucha*
Sexes alike. Cloud forest, Venezuela to Bolivia.

Magpie-Tanager (*Cissopis leveriana*), in which both sexes have
blue-black foreparts, black wings, and a long, graduated black
tail, which contrast with their pure white back, rump, posterior
underparts, and thighs.

Different from other members of the family in coloration as
well as nesting habits are the twenty-five species of short, stout
tanagers called euphonias (*Euphonia*). Males are mostly steel
blue or violaceous black on the upperparts and throat, with
yellow or orange on the forehead and more or less of the crown,
on the underparts posterior to the throat, and occasionally on
the throat itself. A number of species diverge considerably from
this common pattern. The male Golden-sided Euphonia is glossy
purplish black with a golden yellow patch on each side of his
chest. The male blue-black Chestnut-bellied Euphonia of Brazil
also has yellow only at the sides of his breast. The male Blue-
hooded Euphonia has orange-tawny underparts. The male Olive-
backed Euphonia is olive green above and much like the female,

but his forehead is yellow and hers is chestnut. Female euphonias are always plainer than males, chiefly olive green above and
yellowish below. The chlorophonias (*Chlorophonia*) replace the
euphonias in high mountain forests. They are mainly, as their
name suggests, bright green, trimmed with blue, yellow, and, in
one species, chestnut.

Curiously, in a number of anatomical and behavioral features
euphonias resemble the unrelated Mistletoe Bird and its relatives of southern Asia and the Australasian region. All are very
small, rather stout birds with short, fairly thick bills; in both,
the sexes differ in coloration; both have only nine well-devel-
oped remiges, the outermost wing feather being vestigial; both
feed largely on mistletoe berries and are principal disseminators
of the parasitic mistletoe shrubs; and all build nests with a side
entrance, although those of the Mistletoe Birds are pendent instead of supported from below.

Another special group in the tanager family comprises the fifteen species of honeycreepers and dacnises. Long classified with
the flower-piercers and the Bananaquit in another family, the
Coerebidae, they are now regarded as tanagers specialized for extracting nectar from flowers. The flower-piercers have been
transferred to the emberizine finches, leaving the Coerebidae
with only the Bananaquit; for those who classify this widespread
little bird with the wood-warblers, the family has been reduced
to an empty name. The bills of honeycreepers and dacnises are
thinner, sharper, and mostly longer than those of other members
of the family, well suited for probing the corollas of flowers and
extracting nectar with fringed tongue. The bill may be nearly
straight and shorter than the head, as in the dacnises; long and
decurved, as in honeycreepers of the genus *Cyanerpes*; or of intermediate length, as in the Green Honeycreeper.

Dainty, brilliant little birds, male honeycreepers and dacnises
are black and purple, deep blue, turquoise, green, or yellow; the
females are much less richly colored. After the breeding season,
sometimes while still feeding fledglings, the male Red-legged, or
Blue, Honeycreeper changes his blue, turquoise, and black plumage for greenish plumage much like that of females and young,
while retaining his black-and-yellow wing feathers and black

Black-faced Dacnis *Dacnis lineata*
Male. Northern and central South America.

tail. He keeps this "eclipse" plumage for only a few months. Such pronounced seasonal changes of coloration are rare among the constantly resident passerine birds of tropical America—the only other known example is the Blue-black Grassquit. Perhaps it is significant that although the Red-legged Honeycreeper is not a long-distance migrant, it wanders rather widely in flocks after the nesting season.

The nine species of conebills (*Conirostrum*) are small, rather plainly colored birds, which, with the Giant Conebill (the only member of the genus *Oreomanes*), were long placed in the honeycreeper family, then were transferred by some systematists to the wood-warblers, and in the latest classification are included among the tanagers. Confined to tropical South America, with one species ranging into eastern Panama, these birds, which await careful study, are distinguished by their short, sharp bills. The best-known species is the 4.5-inch (11.5-cm) Bicolored Conebill, which is widely distributed east of the Andes. The

Cinereous Conebill *Conirostrum cinereum*
Sexes alike. Andes from Colombia to northern Chile.

male is blue-gray above and light grayish buff below; the female
is grayer above and more yellowish below. The Bicolored Conebill is found chiefly in mangroves and other swampy woodlands, where it gleans insects from foliage and eats berries or
seeds.

Slightly larger and more colorful is the Capped Conebill, of
which the male of one race has a white crown and mostly purplish blue upperparts and black wings, tail, and underparts. The
female's crown and nape are grayish blue, her back olive green,
her underparts yellowish green. This bird, of cloud forest and
humid terrain with scattered low trees, extends from mideleva-
tions to high, treeless Andean paramos. Another conebill of cool
heights is the 7-inch (18-cm) Giant, light gray above, with chestnut eyebrows and underparts and white cheeks and ear coverts.
In the *Polylepis* woods of the high Andes, it climbs over trunks,
searching for insects beneath the bark.

In many parts of tropical America, tanagers are among the
birds most frequently noticed. Brightly colored, rarely given to
skulking in dense vegetation, they do not hide their beauty from
admiring eyes. In tall forests they prefer the upper levels, although a few frequent the undergrowth. They do not shun man;

Black-crowned Palm-Tanager
Phaenicophilus palmarum
Sexes alike. Hispaniola.

indeed they freely enter gardens, parks, and plantations. At least one species, the Blue-gray Tanager, is often seen in towns and cities. Tanagers come readily to feeders where bananas, oranges, or other fruits are offered; over the years, fifteen species, including four honeycreepers, have visited the board in our garden, beside rain forest. Although most abundant on the Central and South American mainland, tanagers occur throughout the Greater and Lesser Antilles, the Bahamas, and Trinidad and Tobago. Five species reside on Hispaniola, three on Puerto Rico, two on Jamaica, and two on Cuba; the Cuban residents include the Red-legged Honeycreeper, a species widespread on the mainland and possibly introduced to the island by man.

2 Food and Foraging

Tanagers prefer a mixed diet of fruits and insects, supplemented by nectar in a number of species. Berries that they can swallow whole are especially attractive. A principal source of such berries is the many species of small and middle-sized trees and shrubs of the melastome family which abound in the rainier parts of tropical America, not only in mature forests but also in second-growth woodlands, in bushy clearings, in hedgerows, and along roadsides. The madder, or coffee, family (Rubiaceae) also contains many shrubs and small trees that supply berries to tanagers and other birds. Small fruits of epiphytic aroids and bromeliads bring variety to the tanagers' diets. In highland forests, epiphytic shrubs of the heath family, which grow profusely on trees in forests and clearings, are a rich source of berries. In almost any locality where tanagers abound, a diligent naturalist can compile a long list of plants whose fruits they eat. On the island of Trinidad, for example, David and Barbara Snow recorded Silver-beaked Tanagers taking the fruits or arillate seeds of thirty-nine species of plants, Bay-headed Tanagers of thirty-three species, and Turquoise Tanagers of twenty-six species.

Tanagers pluck berries while perching or clinging rather than on the wing, in the manner of the manakins that at lower altitudes often forage with them at generously fruiting trees. If the berry is small and thin-skinned, a bird may swallow it whole. If it is larger and tough-skinned, a bird will often mandibulate it, pressing out and swallowing the pulp with included seeds, then dropping the skin. The ground under a tree where Blue-hooded Euphonias were eating mistletoe berries was strewn with parchmentlike husks, from which the entire contents had been neatly removed.

9

Blue-hooded Euphonia *Euphonia elegantissima*
Female (above) and male (below) eating mistletoe
berries. Mexico to western Panama.

If the fruit hanging on a tree or lying on a feeder is too big to be plucked whole, tanagers peck into it. In this manner they nibble on bananas, papayas, and the fruits of the pejibaye palm, which hang in heavy bunches high on trees bristling with long, needle-sharp black spines. Unless pejibaye fruits are well cooked, they sting the mouth unbearably. (Once cooked, however, they are a delicious and nutritious human food.) I have often watched wonderingly while Scarlet-rumped Tanagers, finches, orioles, and other birds ate them.

Another large fruit attractive to birds is the fragrant guava, widely used in the tropics for jellies and desserts. One morning, while I watched a Streaked Saltator pecking into a full-grown but still green guava in the top of a tree beside our house, a male Tawny-bellied, or Spotted-crowned, Euphonia began gathering from the leaves and eating particles of fruit that the larger bird had dropped. Becoming impatient, he moved to the other side of the saltator's guava, clung to it, and started to eat; but he was repulsed with a peck. When he again tried to share the fruit with the saltator, he was permitted to do so; and the two birds, so different in size, ate close together. Soon the saltator flew away; but the euphonia did not long remain in possession of the fruit, because another saltator, apparently the mate of the first, claimed it. After the second saltator was satisfied, the euphonia returned to the guava and ate freely, pecking out bits from the inside and mandibulating them, just as the saltators did. Before the tiny bird had eaten much, a Blue-gray Tanager displaced him at the fruit. The tanager ate little, and after its departure the euphonia resumed his meal, only to be promptly driven away by a Buff-throated Saltator. He had spent much more time waiting than eating.

The tall, spindly cecropia trees—which spring up freely on cleared lands and in forest openings in the humid tropics—attract many birds, including tanagers, with their long, dangling spikes of fruit. The birds hang head downward, stripping off the tiny green fruits that densely cover the cordlike axis, leaving it thin and bare. The brown, furry cushion at the base of each of the cecropia's large, palmately lobed leaves produces a succession of tiny white corpuscles; these are the food of the azteca ants that inhabit the tree's hollow trunk and branches. If all these protein bodies are not promptly removed by the ants, they provide dainty tidbits for small birds, including Golden-masked Tanagers, Bay-headed Tanagers, and euphonias.

Although arillate seeds fall into the broad category of fruits, they are so different from berries and drupes that they require special consideration. An aril is a soft tissue that grows from the base of a seed and partly or wholly envelops it. Singly or in quantity, arillate seeds are produced in pods that may or may not be woody but are usually tough and resistant to the bills of birds. Accordingly, the arils are not available to birds until the capsule opens, in its own good time, by means of two or more spreading valves. Then the arils—white, yellow, orange, red, or black— contrast strongly with the surrounding red, yellow, or brown valves, inviting birds to come and take them. Rich in oil, the arils are poor in starch and sugars. Those I have tasted hardly tempted me to eat them, but birds devour them avidly. Little known in the North Temperate Zone, arillate seeds abound in the tropics. On the Costa Rican farm where I write, they are produced by more than twenty species of trees, shrubs, vines, and stout herbaceous plants; and all are eaten by birds, including sixteen kinds of tanagers.

At generously fruiting trees and shrubs, birds hardly need to compete for berries freely exposed for all to take. At a tree with relatively few large capsules opening one or a few at a time to release highly attractive arils, rivalry may be keen. Of the many species of small trees of the genus *Clusia*, in the family Guttiferae, which grow as epiphytes on larger trees in Costa Rica and whose arillate seeds attract birds, the one with the biggest pods is *Clusia rosea*. Some years ago, a tree of this species flourished on a calabash tree in front of our house, bearing apple-sized fruits amid thick, glossy leaves. The fruits opened by nine to twelve valves that spread outward like the petals of a flower, exposing as many cells packed with small seeds covered by orange-red arils. So great was the birds' eagerness that they would not wait for the pods to open fully but tried to extract seeds through the first narrow fissures of dehiscing capsules. Hanging back-downward or hovering beneath the pods, Red-legged and

Shining honeycreepers inserted their long, slender bills through the chinks and managed to remove arils. They were less successful than woodpeckers, whose stronger bills could force apart the slowly opening valves. While the woodpeckers feasted, the honeycreepers flitted around them, awaiting their turn.

At this clusia tree, a hierarchy developed, with the Golden-naped Woodpeckers at the top. Next came the Red-crowned Woodpeckers, who in turn displaced Green Honeycreepers from the pods. The Green Honeycreepers were dominant over Shining Honeycreepers, who displaced Red-legged Honeycreepers, often the most numerous species. Repeatedly I saw Red-legs of both sexes try, unsuccessfully, to intercept arils that the male Golden-naped Woodpecker was passing to his young. These birds who lost so much time and energy trying to obtain arils were not starving, for bananas awaited them on a feeder a few yards away. Tanagers with bills shorter and thicker than those of honeycreepers were at such a disadvantage at this clusia tree that they hardly tried to compete for the arils, although they freely ate those of clusias with smaller, more abundant pods, as well as arils of many other trees and vines. If an arillate seed is large, the tanager may carry it away whole, to peck off fragments in some secluded spot, as I have seen Gray-headed and Scarlet-rumped tanagers do with seeds of *Protium.*

The chief nectar-drinkers in the tanager family are, of course, the honeycreepers. The long, thin bills and cleft, fringed tongues serve well to extract the sweet liquid from rather open flowers, such as those of the genera *Inga* and *Calliandra* in the tribe Mimoseae, with clusters of long-exserted white or red stamens. Unlike hummingbirds, honeycreepers rarely hover while drinking nectar but perch inward from the flowers and bend over to insert their bills. Red-legged Honeycreepers hang head-downward to a cluster of banana flowers to reach the nectar richly secreted at the bases of the long white tubes. Fragrant white orange blossoms also attract them. Like hummingbirds, honeycreepers can be trained to prefer certain colors placed around tubes of sweetened water. They can discriminate fairly well between adjacent shades in a series of twelve colors.

Although poorly adapted for nectar-drinking, tanagers with

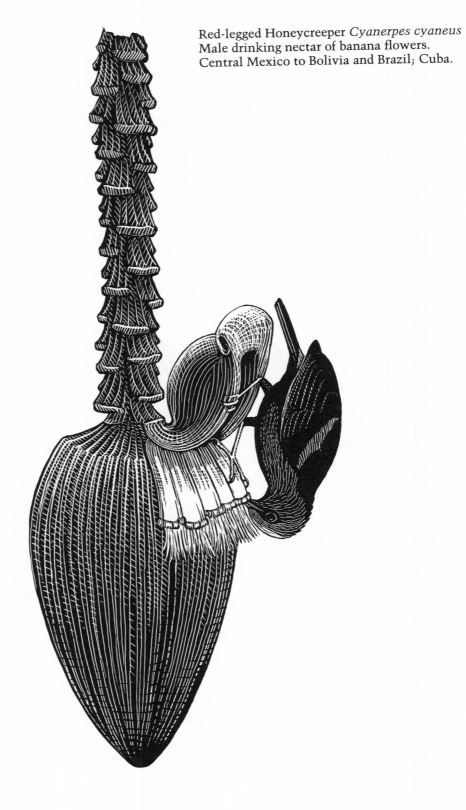

Red-legged Honeycreeper *Cyanerpes cyaneus*
Male drinking nectar of banana flowers.
Central Mexico to Bolivia and Brazil; Cuba.

thicker bills sip nectar when they can. In Suriname, Blue-gray and Palm tanagers share with many other birds the abundant nectar of the orange flowers of the *Erythrina glauca* trees that shade the coffee plantations. Even the tanagers with the stoutest bills, including the Scarlet-rumped of Central America and the Silver-beaked of northern South America, apparently manage to reach some of the sweet secretions in small or open flowers, such as those of the rose-apple tree, the copalchí, and the inga.

In the bright sunshine of a December morning, I watched a pair of Tawny-bellied Euphonias in a clump of tall, slender-stemmed shrubs of the acacialike *Calliandra similis*. The numerous long, thin red stamens sprang in clusters from the little five-toothed green calyces, each of which was brimful of sweet liquid, which, if not pure nectar, was nectar mixed with water from the rain that had fallen in the night, readily accessible even to the short bills of the euphonias. The birds appeared to squeeze the calyces with their bills, to press out nectar they could not reach with their tongues. With them was a Golden-masked Tanager, also enjoying the sweetness.

If nectar is not otherwise accessible, short-billed tanagers may pluck flowers to reach it. High in the mountains of Guatemala, I watched Common Bush-Tanagers among the shrubby *Salvia nervata*, which grew abundantly in more open parts of the cypress forests. Perching near an inflorescence, a bush-tanager pulled a long crimson corolla from the calyx, mandibulated the basal end, doubtless to press out the nectar, then dropped the corolla. Sometimes, after discarding a corolla, a bird would probe with bill or tongue into what was left of the flower, apparently to glean any nectar that remained. The ground beneath the salvia shrubs was strewn with hundreds of corollas, most of which had been torn off just above the short calyx, leaving a stump attached to the plant. That other corollas, still intact, had not fallen spontaneously was evident from marks that the birds' bills had impressed on the delicate tissue. In Trinidad, White-lined Tanagers pulled flowers from the vine *Norantea* and crushed the base to squeeze the nectar out. Somewhat similarly, Silver-beaked Tanagers tore into the bases of the purple, pealike blossoms of the leguminous vine *Dioclea guianensis*, apparently to reach the nectar.

The epiphytic vine *Marcgravia* bears its flowers in a pendent whorl, beneath the center of which hangs a cluster of cuplike nectaries. In a lowland forest in southern Costa Rica, Green Honeycreepers came all day long, often four or five at a time, to cling to these cups and extract something from them, probably both nectar and insects attracted to it; but the *Marcgravia* inflorescences hung so high in a treetop that I could not distinguish details. Golden-naped Woodpeckers, Crowned Woodnymph Hummingbirds, and wintering Baltimore Orioles shared the nectar with the honeycreepers.

As pollinators, honeycreepers and other tanagers appear to play a minor role except possibly at flowers with long stamens projecting in clusters, like those of *Inga, Calliandra,* and species of the myrtle family, including the introduced rose-apple tree. As disseminators of plants with small fruits or arillate seeds that they can swallow whole, including melastomes, clusias, and many others, tanagers are of first importance. Euphonias are the principal carriers from tree to tree of mistletoe seeds, which, when voided, are surrounded by a colorless mucilage that attaches them to branches, where they germinate. However, euphonias are by no means the only dispersers in tropical America of mistletoes, whose little fruits are eagerly devoured by larger tanagers, flycatchers, pigeons, and many other birds. Trees with large fruits or large seeds, such as those of many species of the laurel and nutmeg families, are disseminated mostly by birds bigger than tanagers, including toucans, trogons, and cotingas. Usually tanagers peck fragments of white arils from the fairly large seeds of *Dipterodendron* and *Protium,* without removing them from their open pods; occasionally, however, they carry the whole seed away, to eat the aril at a distance and perhaps drop the seed where it will grow into another tree, as already told of the Gray-headed Tanager.

In addition to eating soft fruits, arils, and nectar, some tanagers vary their diets with green leaves and shoots. For a decade, a pair of Blue-gray Tanagers came frequently to eat leaves of the leguminous *Cassia indecora* in front of our kitchen window. A straggling native shrub that scrambled into a tree, it displayed a profusion of yellow flowers early in the dry season. Tearing off small pieces of young leaflets, the tanagers mashed them in their bills before swallowing them. Less often a Scarlet-rumped Tanager would eat this green salad. The green flowers and tender young fruits of vines of the cucumber family are also often taken by tanagers.

At a hotel on the island of Tobago, Blue-gray Tanagers, White-lined Tanagers, and Red-crowned Woodpeckers came throughout the day to sugar bowls. Such addiction to sugar had long been known of Bananaquits but seems not to have been previously recorded of tanagers. Apparently, these two species of tanagers developed their taste for sugar after the hurricane of September 1963, which stripped much of the foliage from trees and shrubs and made food so scarce that birds thronged around houses in search of it. Blue-gray Tanagers are certainly more comfortable with man on the islands than on the mainland, where everywhere I have found them shy and distrustful.

Probably all tanagers include insects, spiders, and other small invertebrates in their diet, in proportions that vary with the species. Often they search for mature and larval insects amid living foliage, especially that clustered at the ends of twigs, or they investigate curled dead leaves caught up in vine tangles. Sharp-clawed Palm Tanagers hang head-downward while they look for small creatures on hard, slippery palm fronds. Occasionally, tanagers dart out into the air to seize flying insects, a method of foraging that they are most likely to use when, after a shower, a slowly fluttering winged brood of termites fills the evening air. Often tanagers hunt over mossy or lichen-covered branches, sometimes pulling off pieces of these small plants to see what lurks beneath. A common method of foraging, frequently followed by species of *Tangara* and *Thraupis*, is to move deliberately along a horizontal tree limb an inch or more thick and to bend far down, now on one side, now on the other, seeking small creatures amid moss and lichens on the underside.

White-vented Euphonias have a similar procedure, practiced chiefly on slender dead twigs, the thickness of a lead pencil or less, in exposed treetops. By hopping or sidling along, or about-facing alternately to right and left, with each reversal of direction bringing the foot that was behind to the front, they advance outward along the twigs, bending down to examine the undersides for creatures that are nearly always too small to be detected from the ground. As they proceed in this deliberate fashion, they incessantly wag their half-spread tails slowly from side to side. Shining Honeycreepers search methodically over thin dead or nearly leafless dangling vines, hanging in all attitudes by their prominent yellow feet while they glean tiny insects and spiders. In the same fashion, they sometimes diligently explore thin, exposed, leafless twigs of trees. The related Red-legged Honeycreepers more often hunt, warblerlike, amid the terminal foliage of twigs.

Beneath dense thickets and canebrakes, Rosy Thrush-Tanagers forage over the ground, flicking aside fallen leaves with their strong bills; in dry weather these shy birds, who when silent are difficult to detect, rustle the litter loudly enough to disclose their presence. Insects and other small invertebrates, together with fallen berries and seeds, probably reward their diligent leaf-tossing. Another ground-forager is the little-known Chat-Tanager of Hispaniola. Habitual ground-foraging is rare in this arboreal family, but Scarlet-rumped Tanagers, Silver-beaks, and Common Bush-Tanagers occasionally descend to lawns or grassy roadsides for grasshoppers, crickets, or other food. In northern woodlands, Scarlet Tanagers sometimes hop over the ground searching for insects. On cool days in early spring, they follow the plow with American Robins and blackbirds, gathering earthworms, grubs, ants, and ground beetles—surprising fare for tanagers.

The wide-ranging Gray-headed Tanagers, the only species in the genus *Eucometis*, forage mainly with army ants, especially the multitudinous legions of *Eciton burchelli*. The birds catch the roaches, spiders, and other invertebrates that expose themselves as they flee from the ravenous hexapod horde, rather than the ants themselves. These tanagers generally accompany the ants in pairs, often with one or two well-grown young. Nervous and shy, constantly twitching wings and tail while they repeat a subdued *chip*, they fade into the undergrowth in the presence of a human observer, while bolder ant-followers, such as the Bicolored Antbird, continue to forage with the ants. When these purveyors of food are hard to find, Gray-headed Tanagers may seek others. Once, for the better part of an hour, a pair remained

close to a party of domestic chickens industriously scratching
at the forest's edge. At intervals the tanagers alighted on the
ground where a hen had just scattered the litter or flew from
perch to perch above the chickens, apparently to catch flying insects that the domestic fowls had stirred up. As one expects of
ant-followers, Gray-headed Tanagers depend less on fruits and
more on insects than other members of the family. I did not see
them eat bananas at our board until early in the same dry season
during which they foraged with the chickens instead of army
ants, twenty years after the feeder had been put into operation.
At fruit trees, they are seen less often than other tanagers. Red-
throated Ant-Tanagers and Black-cheeked Ant-Tanagers also
persistently follow army ants, but Red-crowned Ant-Tanagers do
so only rarely.

When a swarm of army ants comes to the forest's edge, or beyond, into a neighboring bushy opening, other birds, not profes-
sional ant-followers, may profit by the situation, augmenting
their diet with readily caught insects. In these circumstances,
Scarlet-rumped Tanagers and White-lined Tanagers forage with
the ants.

Another member of the family with special ways of foraging is
the Summer Tanager, which preys heavily on the tender larvae
and pupae of wasps, both in open vespiaries such as those of *Pol-
istes* and in the closed structures of many tropical species. The
birds tear off the papery envelopes of the closed vespiaries before
extracting the larvae. Many of the curious nests that wasps build
on the walls and exposed beams of our house and outbuildings
are ruined after the Summer Tanager arrives in October. Sometimes a scratching on the outer wall of my study, while I sit
writing or reading inside, is my first intimation that the Summer Tanager has returned to us and is tearing apart a vespiary.
Expert aerial flycatchers, Summer Tanagers often seize domestic
bees as they fly to and from their hives, sometimes so many that
beekeepers are led to shoot them. In both their summer and winter homes, Summer Tanagers attack wasp's nests and devour
honeybees.

On rare occasions, tanagers eat small vertebrates. Once I
watched a female Scarlet-rumped Tanager try to swallow a little

Summer Tanager *Piranga rubra*
Male eating a bee. United States and northern
Mexico; in winter to Bolivia and Amazonian Brazil.

Anolis lizard, already dead, but she carried it beyond view before
I could learn the outcome of this effort. Another female Scarlet-
rumped Tanager picked from the ground a pink, naked newborn
mouse that had fallen from a box of old papers I was cleaning
out and fed it to a nestling. Versatile tanagers are generalists
rather than specialists in foraging.

3 Voice

Tanagers are more famous for their plumage than for their voices. Because they are colorful birds that live mostly in open country or in the upper levels of woodland where the light is strong, and because they usually are not very territorial and often are paired throughout the year, they have less need of song to proclaim territory, attract mates, and maintain contact with their partners than do, for example, the neutrally colored wrens that forage in dense vegetation where visibility is limited. Despite their generally poor reputation as songsters, tanagers range from species that appear to be quite songless to those that sing enchantingly.

Let us begin with the dainty little honeycreepers. One of the loveliest and most vocal is the turquoise-crowned male Red-legged, whose most frequent note is a thin, weak, nasal *chaa*. Like a number of American flycatchers and other poor songsters, his singing, if it may be called that, is restricted largely to the dawn. Then, in the nesting season, amid the darkly clustered foliage of the treetop where, apparently, he has roosted, he gives for many minutes a performance of the utmost simplicity, devoid of musical quality. *Tsip tsip chaa, tsip tsip chaa, tsip tsip chaa*, he repeats over and over, punctuating his clearer notes with his usual call, until growing daylight silences him. Even simpler was the only sustained vocal performance I ever heard from the related Shining Honeycreeper, who, late on a drizzly September afternoon, for a quarter of an hour monotonously repeated the same slight note, devoid of melody. From a pair of Shining Honeycreepers, whose nesting I watched from the beginning, I heard no sound until the nestlings were about to leave, when the parents protested my presence below them with a low, rapidly repeated metallic *click* or *tick*. From Green Honeycreepers, numerous for years around our house, I have never heard anything remotely resembling a song. Their usual note is a sharp, wood-warbler-like *chip;* when perturbed, they emit a low, dry rattle. From the Blue Dacnis I have heard only slight, weak monosyllables and lisping notes. The Scarlet-thighed Dacnis appears to be no more vocal.

It is difficult to find information about the many elegant callistes, but none of the better-known species ranks high as a songster. From Silver-throated Tanagers, which for years have nested in our garden, I have heard only a dry, nasal buzz and other weak, insectlike sounds. A sharp, dry *tick,* rapidly repeated by both sexes, whether at rest or in flight, is the usual note of Golden-masked Tanagers; it appears to serve chiefly to maintain contact between a male and female of these continuously mated birds. At daybreak through a long nesting season, this lusterless *tick* may be repeated with sufficient persistence and frequency to be considered a tuneless dawn song. The note of the Speckled Tanager, similar to that of the Golden-masked but more resonant and bell-like, may be repeated with increasing rapidity until it becomes almost a trill, then tapers off to a sharp point. As far as I have heard, Plain-colored Tanagers do not compensate for their grayness by singing brightly. Among the callistes, the best songster I have heard is the Bay-headed Tanager. The male's song consists of four or five notes descending in pitch with a most peculiar whining twang—a slight, simple, but appealing effort. The Turquoise Tanager, which I have not heard, voices a high-pitched, squeaky chatter, usually by several birds together.

Plainly attired, olive green Common Bush-Tanagers of highland forests are no better songsters than the more colorful species of *Tangara.* As they fly about in pairs at the approach of the breeding season or pursue rivals, they rapidly repeat sharp, twittering notes. This tuneless utterance should probably be considered their song, for at dawn it is sometimes continued, with hardly a pause, for as much as half an hour.

Among the foregoing vocally poor tanagers and honeycreepers, the same basic note, variously modified, serves most of the functions of voice. Thus, the Golden-masked Tanager's *tick* is used to maintain contact, to compose a simple song, or, rapidly repeated, to express anxiety or anger when the nest appears to be imperiled.

Song improves when we pass to the genus *Thraupis*. The animated song of the male Blue-gray Tanager is varied and intricate, revealing a certain musical virtuosity; but the tone is weak and slightly squeaky. The bird seems to be attempting a song beyond his slight vocal power. His mate occasionally delivers a song briefer and weaker than his. Their call note is a long-drawn, slightly squeaky monosyllable, in tone quality much like the song. The song of the related Palm Tanager is similar to that of the Blue-gray but less sustained.

Hardly brilliant musicians, tanagers of the colorful genus *Ramphocelus* have appealing, simple songs that they do not stint. In voices that range from full and rich to slighter and weaker, male Scarlet-rumped Tanagers repeat, tirelessly at dawn in the breeding season and less profusely at intervals through the day, a phrase of two or three pleasant notes. I have never heard a female of this abundant species sing. The most common call of Scarlet-rumped Tanagers is a nasal *ac* or *wac*, very different in tone from the song. While his mate built a nest, a male Crimson-backed Tanager in Panama sang, charmingly, *sweet you do; sweet you do, you do*. The Silver-beak, widespread in northern South America, sings as fluently as the two related species, but often in a thinner, squeakier voice. Occasionally, in some secluded spot, a male indulges in a whisper song, or subsong—a finchlike flow of slight, varied musical notes—a delightful medley such as I have heard from no other tanager. The song of the Crimson-collared Tanager of Central America is a leisurely sequence of rising and falling notes, simple but pleasant.

In the genus *Piranga*, vocal ability shows further improvement. The song of the male Scarlet Tanager is a continuous flow of short phrases, alternately high and low in pitch, in form not unlike the American Robin's song but distinguished by a slightly hoarse or throaty burr. The female Scarlet Tanager sings much like the male, but often in a softer voice, while she gathers materials for her nest or food for her young. Sometimes the members of a mated pair sing to each other with verses that differ little. The Summer Tanager's song is similar to that of the

Scarlet Tanager but louder, faster, more musical. In autumn, soon after the Summer Tanager's arrival in tropical America, lilting snatches of this song may be heard when two individuals contend for a winter territory. The Summer Tanager's call, *chicky-tucky-tuck*, bears no resemblance to its song. The male Flame-colored Tanager, resident in the highlands of Mexico and Central America, has a song much like that of the Summer Tanager, melodious in spite of a touch of harshness or huskiness in the full, deep notes. One male sang *chewee-very-vire*, the *very* lowest in pitch, the final *vire* abruptly higher. His somewhat throaty voice suggested midsummer lushness. The call of this tanager, a full-voiced *prr-rt prr-rt*, is quite different from its song.

The song of the male Gray-headed Tanager, prolonged, complex, always sweetly soft, is one of the finest I have heard from any tanager and would win praise for a thrush. He sings rather sparingly while foraging with army ants in the undergrowth of tropical forests, while helping his mate build a nest, and while perching well above the ground, sometimes almost to midheight of the taller trees. One version sounded like *whichis whichis whicheery whichís whichú*. Sometimes the song is even longer and more elaborate, flowing smoothly from verse to verse, now and again rising to a jubilant crescendo. The call is a subdued *chip*.

The Rosy Thrush-Tanager's full, mellow tones would make this bird an outstanding songster in any avian family. Its short, varied phrases, each repeated several times in rapid succession in the manner of mockingbirds and thrashers, are wonderfully sweet. Usually they fail to suggest words, but one male sang quite distinctly to his mate, *Don't fret, dearie; cheer, cheer, cheerily cheer*. Living in dense vegetation where visibility is reduced, a male and female (who appear to live in pairs throughout the year) maintain contact vocally. With a voice only a little less full and strong than his, she joins him in duets or calls responsively with him. Despite their liquid sweetness the thrush-tanager's call notes are often reiterated until they become monotonous. One, a rather querulous *queo* (or *kweeo*), tirelessly repeated on cloudy afternoons, suggested the name "queo" for this bird, whose classification has puzzled ornithologists because it is not a typical tanager.

In ant-tanagers (*Habia*), voice is well developed and freely used, as though to compensate for the subdued red of these birds that frequent the poorly lighted lower levels of tropical woodlands. As noisy Red-crowned Ant-Tanagers progress rapidly through the underwood, usually with companions of other species, they keep up a constant chatter of incongruously mixed harsh and pleasantly soft notes. On rare occasions, the male warbles softly and sweetly, a performance of singular beauty seldom long continued; one sang in this manner as he approached his nest with food in his bill. At dawn during the long breeding season in southern Costa Rica, the male Red-crowned Ant-Tanager hides in a dense thicket, often at the forest's edge, monotonously repeating, for many minutes, in a clear, crisp voice, either *peter, peter, peter* or a trisyllable that sounds like *peter-bird, peter-bird*, or, perhaps, *intervene, intervene.*

On the Pacific slope of Guatemala, male Red-crowned Ant-Tanagers, who lurked all day in the dense vegetation of deep ravines between ridges planted with coffee, rose at daybreak to sing their dawn songs high in the trees that shaded the coffee shrubs, sometimes on the topmost boughs. For the better part of an hour they would repeat a song, lovely in its simplicity, of from seven to nine loud, clear notes, with considerable pauses between repetitions. From well-separated treetops the songsters appeared to answer one another with verses that showed great individuality, forming a dawn chorus worthy of thrushes. While singing, the ant-tanagers often spread their usually concealed scarlet crown-patches, which shone brightly even in the half-light of dawn. Finally, as daylight waxed, they dived straight downward, almost seeming to fall, into the deep ravines where their mates nested. While the sun is high, the dawn songs of Red-crowned Ant-Tanagers are heard only in territorial disputes or, perhaps, in the excitement of escape from a predator.

Although the scoldings, or call notes, of Red-throated Ant-Tanagers are exceptionally harsh, their song has received high praise for its musical quality. Consisting sometimes of as many as sixteen clear, flutelike notes, it is heard not only at daybreak but throughout the day, more often than the corresponding song of the Red-crown. Often the refrain *glad to meet you* stands out clearly in repetitions of this arrestingly beautiful song. What a contrast between the voices of the least and most vocally gifted species in this great family!

I have left until last the voices of euphonias, not because they are the best songsters among tanagers but because certain special features of their singing, as of their nesting, set them apart from other members of the family. Their performances—usually medleys of whistles and soft, liquid notes, frequently in doublets and triplets and often mixed with various harsh, dry, or throaty notes—are notable for duration rather than high musical quality. The song of the Blue-hooded Euphonia, one of the better songsters, is a prolonged, rambling sequence of weak, tinkling notes, alternately high and low, tumbling over one another without a definite pattern. A flock of mixed ages and sexes, all eating mistletoe berries in a high treetop, produce a wild but delightfully cheery disharmony of many voices. In such social singing, Blue-hooded Euphonias resemble siskins.

Perching inconspicuously in a tree, early in the dry season, when the air is fresh and flowers abound, a male Tawny-bellied Euphonia may continue for a quarter of or even half an hour, with hardly a pause, to pour forth various combinations of short notes that may be either clear or dry and chaffy. One male sang *chip a cher weet*, the first and last syllables accented. A series of drier notes sounded like *chip tuck tuck*, with emphasis on the *chip*. While the male chants his pleasantly artless medley, the female may answer with a dry *churr*. At other times her song resembles that of the male.

No less notable for duration than their songs are the complaints of euphonias when their nests are disturbed or destroyed. A female Tawny-bellied Euphonia, whose nest hung low above a pool in a mountain torrent where I often bathed, would protest the whole time I was in the water. Another female of this species, whose eggs had just been eaten by a squirrel, continued for a quarter of an hour, with hardly a pause, to repeat a rapid, throaty *churr*, punctuated at intervals by a sharp *chip chip chip*. While complaining, she turned from side to side and flipped out her short wings, both together. Finally, she ate a berry from a nearby shrub and flew away with her mate.

Although not the best songsters, euphonias include the only

Thick-billed Euphonia *Euphonia laniirostris*
Male perched on an epiphytic aroid,
Anthurium scandens. Costa Rica to Bolivia
and Amazonian Brazil.

mimics so far reported in the tanager family. As one would expect from the character of their own songs, they tend to imitate
the call and alarm notes, rather than the melodious verses, of
their neighbors. Songs of Violaceous Euphonias on Trinidad consisted of a rapid warbling, interspersed with a rolling *chree* and
an occasional staccato *bee bee.* These songs might be delivered
without imitations or be diversified by the inclusion of notes of
seventeen species in ten families—not all, of course, in a single
performance. Among the sounds reproduced were the flight call
of a parrot; alarm notes of anis, antbirds, and house wrens; the
kiskadee call of the Great Kiskadee; and the squeal of a Silver-
beaked Tanager being removed from a mist net for banding.
Only males were heard to imitate other birds.

In Amazonia, Thick-billed Euphonias may sing without imitations or may compose songs wholly of notes borrowed from
other species, from harsh screams to soft calls. The models include birds as different as hawks, jacamars, toucans, woodpeckers, woodcreepers, antbirds, flycatchers, vireos, tanagers,
orioles, and flinches—a total of twenty-five species, all mim-
icked with such accuracy that the reproductions are hardly dis-
tinguishable from the originals. In Panama, female Thick-billed
Euphonias, driven from their nests, imitate notes that neighboring birds would use in similar circumstances; on two occasions
they incited a Yellow-green Vireo to scold the person who had
disturbed them.

Could it be that the Violaceous and Thick-billed euphonias
developed mimicry, especially of alarm notes, to gain support
from other birds when their nests were in peril? And could they
later have added a more varied repertoire of borrowed sounds to
their songs?

Perhaps when we know more of the songs of the tanagers that
live deep in Amazonian forests and on precipitous Andean
slopes, we will be compelled to modify the view that the family
is, in general, poorly endowed with song.

4 Daily Life

While seeking food in forests, thickets, or plantations or at feeders, tanagers reveal much about their social arrangements. Blue-gray Tanagers, Palm Tanagers, Gray-headed Tanagers, and many callistes fly and forage in pairs at all seasons and probably keep the same partner as long as both live. The young may separate from their parents soon after they become proficient foragers, or they may stay with them for months, forming closely knit groups of three, four, or five.

After the breeding season several pairs may join to form larger flocks in which pairs are not evident (as they often are evident in flocks of macaws and other parrots), although they may well persist. Individuals, pairs, and larger groups of tanagers frequently join in mixed flocks of birds of different species, families, and orders which wander through humid forests, each foraging in its own way. On the wooded lower slopes of the Andes in Colombia, Ecuador, and eastern Peru, these flocks may contain a bewildering array of small tanagers of the most diverse color patterns. A frequent association throughout the length of Central America is that of Red-crowned Ant-Tanagers and Tawny-crowned Greenlets; the latter, members of the vireo family, are half the tanagers' size. The two move rapidly through lower levels of the forest, often accompanied by such other birds as Slaty Antwrens, Sulphur-rumped Flycatchers, and Buff-throated Automoluses.

Scarlet-rumped Tanagers, Silver-beaked Tanagers, and other species of *Ramphocelus* wander through bushy fields and pastures, plantations, and gardens in flocks so loose and straggling that it is difficult to ascertain the number of their members. The flocks often appear to contain about a dozen individuals of both sexes, with females predominating. Through dense thickets scarcely penetrable by man, at the edges of lowland rain forests, and at marshy openings in their midst, chattering families of six, eight, or, rarely, more Dusky-faced Tanagers move restlessly. Unlike many other tanagers, these cooperatively breeding birds of thickets and bushy clearings (see chapter 10) seldom travel with other species.

Tanagers probably preen as much as other birds but do so amid sheltering foliage, where they are rarely seen. Like toucans, they prefer to bathe in elevated pools, such as those in cavities of trunks and branches, rather than at ground level. One morning I watched a female Red-legged Honeycreeper in a guava tree shaking and preening her dripping feathers. After she flew away, a female Green Honeycreeper bathed in rainwater that had collected in a decay-formed cavity in the cut-off end of a thick, ascending branch. The green bird repeatedly immersed herself in this little aerial pool, then stood on the rim to arrange her soaked plumage. Another Green Honeycreeper bathed in the wa-

White-rumped Tanager *Cypsnagra hirundinacea*
Sexes alike. Brazil, Paraguay, and Bolivia.

ter between the broad leaves, forming a rosette, of an epiphytic tank bromeliad. I have also watched Silver-throated Tanagers dip themselves in pools on high, decaying boughs.

A pair of Speckled Tanagers approached a silken nest that small, blackish spinning ants had woven in the clustered green leaves of a tree, using their thread-secreting larvae as the source of silk. From the surface of the nest and surrounding foliage and twigs, the speckled birds plucked ant after ant, each of which they rubbed along the inner, or lower, surface of a raised wing, in the common avian activity called "anting." After using the ants in this manner, the birds swallowed them. Sometimes one of the tanagers appeared to rub an ant on the underside of its forwardly tilted tail, and sometimes it appeared to eat one without first touching the plumage with it—the swiftness of the birds' movements, the height of the ants' nest, and interfering foliage made it difficult to distinguish details. For several minutes both members of the pair continued to treat ant after ant in this fashion, while the little insects stood upright on their nest—as is their habit when threatened—and by striking their abdomens against it doubtless made a rustling sound that I was too far away to hear above the clamor of the neighboring mountain torrent. Then, rapidly repeating their little bell-like notes, the pair flew away, leaving me wondering about the purpose of this behavior, for which various explanations have been offered; one is that it applies parasite-repellent formic acid to the feathers.

I have repeatedly seen Green Honeycreepers and Blue-gray Tanagers anting, much as the Speckled Tanagers did, and always in trees. The ants that tropical tanagers use for this activity are mostly small, stingless species, such as the spinning ants and azteca ants that inhabit the hollow trunks of cecropia trees. The foregoing episodes of anting lasted a few minutes at most; but in Pennsylvania two Scarlet Tanagers indulged in this behavior for over an hour, on the ground. Although in the North Temperate Zone birds commonly ant on the ground, with the single exception of an Oriole-Blackbird in Venezuela, all the numerous episodes of anting that I have watched in tropical America, involving fourteen species of seven families, occurred in trees or shrubs, even when the actor was the terrestrial Buff-rumped Warbler.

As birds go about their daily affairs, they sometimes meet a hawk, an owl, a snake, or some other predator of birds or their nests, and they pause to protest the menacing presence. The cries of the first discoverer draw other birds of various species, until the object of dislike is surrounded by a motley mob, complaining in many different sharps and flats. A frequent participant in these mobbing episodes is the Green Honeycreeper, the least gentle member of the tanager family that I know. One of these honeycreepers was among the birds that gathered around a somnolent Spectacled Owl that rested by day high in a forest tree. The owl's great head and massive body, exaggerated by puffed-out plumage, appeared huge beside the smaller birds that flitted around it. The male Green Honeycreeper approached closer to the impassive owl than did the trogons, also members of the mobbing party, but not so near as the diminutive hummingbirds.

Sometimes a lone Green Honeycreeper undertakes to watch a potentially dangerous bird or snake. One June morning a Double-toothed Kite perched, leisurely preening, in the top of a dead tree at the forest's edge. About a yard behind the raptor, on a slender branch, was a male Green Honeycreeper, facing the much bigger kite. For nearly half an hour he remained there, conspicuous against the sky, always with his bill toward the preening kite. That the honeycreeper stayed to watch the kite was evident from his growing restlessness; he fidgeted from side to side, stretched his wings, occasionally preened a little himself. Finally, his patience exhausted, he abandoned his vigil and flew away, leaving the phlegmatic kite in the same spot, where it was present an hour later. Although its food is mainly insects caught in the air, the Double-toothed Kite is not above eating a small bird or pillaging a nest.

On a cloudy afternoon, repeated low, sharp rattles of a male Green Honeycreeper in the spreading mango tree beside my study caused me to drop my pen and go out to investigate. After much peering up into the dense cluster of leaves toward which the bird's scolding was directed, I detected part of the shiny body of a green tree snake, resting well above my head. To protect the birds' nests in the garden, I remove intruding snakes; so I went for my rifle and shot twice at this one. The serpent did not budge. With a long pole I shook the branch where it rested. Still the snake remained immobile. Further investigation revealed that the supposed snake was only a longitudinally curled green leaf, wet and shiny from a recent shower. Apparently, the honeycreeper, who had a much closer view than I did, mistook it for a snake; and I was misled by him. I have not known any other bird to be deceived by a leaf or vine that resembled a snake or part of one.

Honeycreepers are not the only tanagers that engage in mobbing, but I will postpone consideration of the others until chapter 11, which deals with the enemies of birds.

With one known exception, tanagers roost—singly, in pairs, or in larger gatherings of one or more species—in the foliage of trees or in low, dense thickets. The Scarlet-rumped Tanagers on our farm dive at nightfall into the impenetrable tangle of wiry, forking fronds of the scrambling fern *Dicranopteris pectinata* on the hillside behind our house. Mated Blue-gray Tanagers and Golden-masked Tanagers often roost amid the dark foliage of an orange tree, the partners sleeping as far apart as their own length to a foot or more—never in close contact, as anis and many other highly social birds sleep. Silver-throated Tanagers, who are less closely associated with their mates, roost farther from them. Three Silver-throats that I observed over time roosted alone, with no partner nearby. One slept six feet (2 m) above the ground on the petiole of a dracaena shrub, close beneath a broad, arching red-and-green leaf that formed its roof on rainy nights. The second roosted about ten feet (3 m) up on a branch of a flame-of-the-forest tree, where it was well screened above by the foliage but fully exposed below. For several nights the third Silver-throat slept in a flowering shrub, with a Rufous-tailed Hummingbird brooding two nestlings only a foot (30 cm) in front of the tanager's yellow breast.

Sometimes a tanager roosts on a long, stout thorn projecting horizontally from the trunk or an upright branch of an orange tree. For at least a month in the rainy season a Bay-headed Tanager slept this way, its feathers fluffed out, its head turned back and buried in their soft depths; in my flashlight's beam it was an object of brilliant green against the dark verdure of the tree.

Birds that raise their families in open nests rarely use such nests as dormitories, but those that breed in roofed nests, holes, or crannies frequently sleep in them. Accordingly, it is not surprising that euphonias—which, along with chlorophonias, are the only tanagers known to build covered nests—are the only members of the tanager family known to sleep in more sheltered locations than amid foliage. Except when incubating eggs or brooding nestlings, however, they do not seem to pass the night in nests that they have made.

A row of calabash trees stood for many years at the top of the high bank in front of our house, their rough-barked trunks and long, stiff branches covered with clusters of nearly sessile leaves and laden with a rich variety of epiphytes—from mosses, liverworts, and lichens to orchids, aroids, bromeliads, and even small trees. Tawny-bellied Euphonias, sometimes several simultaneously, slept in this exuberant epiphytic growth, usually in pockets in thick brown cushions of the liverwort *Frullania*, which, if they had been lined, would have served as nests for breeding. No more than one individual ever occupied a pocket. In a flashlight's beam, only the yellow breast of a male or the tawny ventral plumage of a female would be visible in the narrow opening. Sometimes, instead of roosting in a nook in the liverworts, a euphonia would sleep among the closely clustered, slender stems of a small orchid growing on the tree, beneath a sheltering mass of the liverwort.

One male euphonia found a sheltered roost on the root of an epiphyte, or perhaps it was the rhizome of a fern, which was stretched an inch or so beneath a horizontal branch overgrown with liverworts. The narrow space between the root and the branch seemed difficult to enter, but the tiny bird shot into it so swiftly and deftly that I could not see how he did it. With his head turned back and his ventral plumage fluffed out, he looked, in my flashlight's beam, like a little ball of bright yellow feathers. He slept with only one foot grasping the perch, the other drawn up and hidden in the yellow mass. (This way of roosting is rather frequent among birds; by exposing less featherless surface, it probably saves a little of the body's heat on cool nights.) The sleeper's back was pressed against the branch at a point where a luxuriant growth of the liverwort formed a wide, spongy brown roof above him during the height of the rainy season.

For a dozen years, until the calabash trees died and fell, the Tawny-bellied Euphonias slept intermittently in them, sometimes a single individual, sometimes a male and a female a few feet apart, and, for long intervals, two males and a female in the same tree. On some evenings, the birds went silently to rest. On others, they perched near their dormitories and for many minutes poured forth an almost continuous stream of either dry, rattling notes or, less often, clearer whistles before they darted into their cozy nooks. In the dim light of dawn, they silently shot out and away.

For nearly two years, with occasional absences, a female Tawny-bellied Euphonia lodged in a large tuft of the brown liverwort hanging beneath a horizontal bough ten feet (3 m) above the lawn. Sometimes her absences were inexplicable; at other times they were caused by a Bananaquit. Throughout the year the tiny, yellow-breasted Bananaquits tirelessly build a succession of snug covered nests, not only for their eggs and young but also as dormitories, in which each sleeps alone. Occasionally they lose a nest and, until they can build another, try to occupy that of some other small bird, often a flycatcher. One day I noticed that a Bananaquit had arranged straws around the doorway of the pocket where the female euphonia had been lodging for many months, thereby contracting the orifice. On arriving that evening, the euphonia paused, clinging to the front of her bedroom, repeating a queer *churr*. When she tried to enter, the yellow-breasted intruder greeted her with pecks. Nevertheless, she persisted in pushing in until she and the Bananaquit tumbled out, locked together, and fell to the ground. Promptly separating, they flew up to the pocket at the same time; again they grappled and dropped to the ground. Finally, the euphonia returned alone and stayed the night. But in the following days the Bananaquit added so much material in front of the pocket that the aperture was drastically reduced, and the euphonia relinquished her sleeping quarters to the intruder.

5 Displays and Disputes

Even in the most harmonious groups, conflicts occasionally arise, and the peaceable tanagers are no exception to this rule. As is true of many other birds, their differences tend to be settled by visual or vocal displays instead of by crude fighting. The most elaborate and prolonged displays I have seen in the tanager family were those of Red-legged Honeycreepers, who are exceptional not only in their method of settling disputes but also in the eclipse plumage of their adult males (see chapter 1).

The quarrels I have seen Red-legged Honeycreepers engage in were always between two individuals of the same sex, more often females than males. Sometimes, while two females disputed, one or two males looked on passively, and birds of other species gathered around as interested spectators. Often, however, the contestants were quite alone. Facing each other on perches a few inches apart, they bowed up and down, pivoted from side to side, twitched wings and tails, and monotonously repeated their calls. Although they frequently flitted from twig to twig, each consistently faced its adversary a foot or less away. Males often elevated their bills and threw their wings outward and upward, flashing yellow from the undersides; or they spread their wings more widely for a second or so, displaying large expanses of yellow (which females lack). The sound most frequently uttered in these encounters is the nasal *chaa* call note, which after a while may change to the clear little *tsip* that enters prominently into the dawn song. Or the two notes may be mixed together, while the contestants continue tirelessly to sway their bodies and twitch their wings and tails. On rare occasions the two rise up and up in the air, hovering face to face on rapidly beating wings, but soon they descend to resume their altercation on perches.

Capped Conebill *Conirostrum albifrons*
Male. Venezuela; Andes from Colombia
to Bolivia.

These disputes often last a quarter of an hour to half an hour.
They appear to be, above all, trials of endurance. After many
minutes one of the contestants appears to tire, calling and pos-
turing less, until finally it abandons the field. Sometimes the
victor chases the loser beyond view. If bodily contact occurs,
it is brief and inconsequential. On one occasion two females
seemed to be contending for a male, who appeared to be a disin-
terested spectator of their dispute. Usually, no motive for the
quarrel is evident.

On a feeder crowded to capacity with a multicolored assemblage of tanagers, finches, orioles, and wood-warblers, one Red-
legged Honeycreeper sometimes alights on the back of another;
but I never saw one take this familiarity with a bird of a different species. When two honeycreepers jostle each other too
closely, they may stop eating and face each other, their slender
bills pointing straight upward while they protest with fine nasal
notes. After displaying in this fashion for a few seconds, they
lower their heads and eat, or one may jab at the other and drive
it away. Occasionally one pursues the other for a few inches,
without fighting. Rarely, one honeycreeper, becoming greedy,
tries to keep others off the board, but it is never successful for

long. If it is not promptly submerged by eight or ten of its kind, a bigger bird soon alights beside it, disregarding its puny bluff. When the feeder is less crowded, such displays of intolerance seldom occur, though occasionally two females will face each other across the banana that both are eating, protest with heads tilted high, remain motionless in this attitude for a few seconds, then resume their meals.

Shining Honeycreepers, less gregarious than Red-legged Honeycreepers, appear to lack similarly conspicuous and prolonged displays. They threaten opponents with spread wings but without revealing their undersides, which are not brightly colored like those of male Red-legged Honeycreepers. When these two species interact, mild fighting may erupt. Once, near the large-fruited clusia tree where birds vied keenly for arils from slowly opening capsules, a female Shining Honeycreeper and a female Red-legged Honeycreeper grappled and fell but separated before striking the ground. Then one chased the other until they returned to the clusia tree. There the Red-legged Honeycreeper displayed with nasal *chaa*s, much as she does when disputing with one of her own kind and sex, while her opponent postured silently in front of her. A male of each species watched without interfering. Soon all four flew to a neighboring tree and, as far as I saw, quarreled no more. On a later occasion I watched a female Red-legged Honeycreeper threaten a male Shining Honeycreeper, repeating her nasal notes. Facing her, he leaned backward, prominently displaying his bright yellow legs. Then he fled, with the female in pursuit—which surprised me, as the Shining Honeycreeper is usually dominant over the Red-legged.

The aggressive Green Honeycreeper, which is larger than the Red-legged and Shining honeycreepers and less sociable, frequently tries to drive other small birds from flowers. It has no striking display and avoids actual fights with its own or other species, but it has rude habits, unknown in other members of the tanager family and rare in the whole avian class. One day, in a narrow clearing in a Panamanian forest, several Plain-colored Tanagers were perching in a guava tree when an adult male Green Honeycreeper drove away all except an immature bird, from whom he pulled a few feathers. Then, attacking from below, he seized a leg of the unfortunate tanager. Soon the victim was clinging to its perch by one leg, while the honeycreeper hung from the other, until I threw a stick toward him. After his departure the young tanager regained its perch and sat for a while as though dazed. No reason for this unprovoked attack was evident. On another occasion, at a clusia tree, a Green Honeycreeper seized the wingtip of a Red-legged Honeycreeper, who hung below the assailant's bill with both wings stretched out until it was released.

More often than he seizes other small birds, the male Green Honeycreeper takes firm hold of the tail of a female Green Honeycreeper and hangs on tenaciously, while she tries to pull away, sometimes crying out in what seems to be pain or alarm. Twice I have seen a male grasp the tail of his mate while she was building a nest. One February afternoon, rapidly repeated sharp notes drew my attention to a male Green Honeycreeper who was holding the tail of a protesting female of his kind. When she broke away, three males in adult plumage pursued her closely. Perhaps the male Green Honeycreeper tries to obtain a mate by seizure. But sometimes, in a gentler mood, he resorts to a more usual mode of courting, offering a female berries, which she readily accepts.

The most prolonged dispute I have witnessed among tanagers was between two species of euphonias. When a pair of White-vented Euphonias started to build a nest in the liverworts on the branch of a calabash tree where two male Tawny-bellied Euphonias had long been roosting, one of the latter tried to keep these smaller birds away. Nevertheless, the White-vented Euphonias finished their nest, and the female laid three eggs.

For a while the Tawny-bellied Euphonia seemed to be reconciled to the breeding pair; but after incubation was well advanced, he became more perturbed by their presence, probably because, after an interval of sleeping elsewhere, he wanted to return to his former lodging. As the pair of White-vented Euphonias approached their nest in the late afternoon, he darted at and scattered them. When they tried again to reach their nest, he again drove them away, but in the end they managed to attend their nest. These clashes were repeated on a number of subsequent evenings. Facing each other, the two males turned from side to side, flipping their wings with a slight, rapid motion and twitching their tails. While so displaying, the male Tawny-bellied Euphonia called *r-r-r-ra cha cha* or *cha cha*. The White-vented Euphonia voiced a high-pitched note that reminded me of the Tropical Kingbird's call, sharp *chip*s, and a lower, almost whistled note. At long intervals one male flew at the other, so suddenly and swiftly that I could not see whether they made contact. The endurance of these protagonists was astounding. Bouts of a quarter of an hour were frequent, and sometimes the euphonias continued to call and posture for nearly an hour, with brief intermissions.

Late one evening, after the White-vented Euphonias' nestlings had hatched and the male Tawny-bellied Euphonia had resumed sleeping in the calabash tree, on a branch above the nest, the latter emerged from his nook, rushed at the nestlings' mother as she was about to enter her nest to brood the young birds, and drove her away. He returned to his niche, only to fly out again chasing the female each time she tried to enter the nest. Five times he drove her from her doorway. After some of these attacks the aggressor looked into the nest, without harming the nestlings. After a while the male White-vented Euphonia started to feed the nestlings, but he too was driven away before he could finish. These quarrels always ended when the Tawny-bellied Euphonia entered his own niche to stay; then the female White-vented Euphonia brooded her nestlings, and her mate flew off toward his undiscovered place of rest. As the nestlings grew older, their Tawny-bellied neighbor became less troublesome. They developed rapidly and flew from the nest exceptionally early for euphonias. Despite the noisy turmoil, in all my hours of watching I never saw one of the contestants touch the other.

This interspecific antagonism was unexpected, because for long intervals two adult male Tawny-bellied Euphonias had slept in the small calabash tree without, as far as I saw, any opposition; and birds more often display territorial exclusiveness toward individuals of their own species than toward those of a different species. I never saw the Tawny-bellied Euphonia molest either the tiny Mistletoe Flycatchers who were rearing a brood in a covered nest amid the liverworts of this calabash tree or the Bananaquit who slept in it. At times these diminutive birds, as well as a passing Little Hermit Hummingbird, were interested spectators of the altercations between the two species of euphonias.

The occasional visit of a second pair of White-vented Euphonias to the vicinity of the nest was another cause of excitement. The resident male flew at the intruding male and the resident female at the intruding female. These pursuits were mild; the birds did not clash, and after a little chasing the four would perch for a while not far apart in the nest tree. The visitors soon flew away with all their feathers.

When one Scarlet-rumped Tanager alights beside another who is eating on the birds' table, the two may depress their foreparts and, with slightly open bills, glare at each other for a brief interval, after which they proceed amicably to share the same banana or orange. Even in situations that among other birds might provoke violent conflict, these usually pacific birds do not fight. On one occasion an exceptionally bright-colored female dispossessed a duller female of the nest in which she had been incubating two eggs. When the original owner tried to return to the nest, where the intruder was now sitting, the latter seized her bill and pushed her backward. In hours of watching the duller female being deprived of her nest, I saw no encounters more violent than this one. Sometimes the contestants perched peaceably side by side. The single male who frequented the area was neutral during this quarrel; he perched in a neighboring ceiba tree and sang. Later, he and the dispossessed female, apparently his mate, went elsewhere, leaving the bright female alone. In her stolen nest she incubated three eggs of the double set, hatched one—her own—and reared the nestling, all without a male's help.

On a morning in a later year, two female Scarlet-rumped Tanagers started to build one nest in an orange tree. The following day one of them began a separate nest a yard from the first. Then each of the two pulled materials from her neighbor's incipient nest and carried them to her own. The same piece traveled repeatedly back and forth; a large, fluffy tuft of spider's silk was so attractive to both birds that it passed from one to the other half a dozen times. Meanwhile, a third female Scarlet-rumped Tanager, building a more distant nest, purloined materials from beneath the very bills of the two in the orange tree, without provoking an attack. Each of the three females had a mate, who attentively watched these strange proceedings but took no part in them. Sometimes the two females who were reciprocally pilfering materials would rest for the better part of a minute, facing each other, almost touching, tense, immobile, and silent, each seeming to try to outstare the other; but neither they nor the males fought. Soon, birds of several species, their attention drawn by so much misdirected activity, began exploiting the incipient nests as a public quarry, carrying off the materials to the structures they were building in neighboring trees, with the result that no nest was finished in the orange tree.

The foregoing episodes, so revealing of the Scarlet-rumped Tanagers' pacific nature, are not typical. Mostly, each nesting female goes about her business without interfering with her neighbors. Nevertheless, I have witnessed some surprising exceptions.

More than thirty years ago, after I had dwelt for nearly two decades among these conspicuously abundant tanagers without ever having witnessed more than a brief, inconsequential clash—never a serious fight, even in situations that might arouse violent hostility in different birds—I felt safe in writing, "Song Tanagers [as I then called them] are most peaceable birds, never fighting among themselves." I should have been more cautious; living nature is so unpredictable that in telling about it one should never say "never." On March 24, 1954, the day before this unguarded statement was published in the first volume of *Life Histories of Central American birds* in faraway Berkeley, California, I saw my first real fight between Scarlet-rumped Tanagers. Two resplendent males dropped to the ground from an orange tree and for a while lay tightly clinched together. Then they rolled around, clutching and biting. After about a minute they separated, and one chased the other through the garden and out over the adjoining pasture until they were lost to view. I did not learn the cause of this conflict, which contrasted so strongly with the peaceful tolerance of the three males whose mates were involved in the imbroglio I had watched in another orange tree.

During the next month I saw male Scarlet-rumped Tanagers engage in other protracted pursuits and grappling fights such as I had never witnessed before. In the following decades I witnessed—though only at long intervals, of seven years and then twelve—fights between male Scarlet-rumped Tanagers whom I had been seeing almost daily. Possibly their belligerence was due to a mutant gene that has since been lost from the local population, for in recent years I have noticed no more fighting. Female Scarlet-rumped Tanagers attack each other even more rarely. While one built a nest only four inches (10 cm) from the nest in which another was incubating her eggs, only twice did I see them grapple and fall, then rise promptly and continue their respective occupations close together.

Throughout the year Golden-masked Tanagers travel in pairs, or, less often, three or four adults together. To roost, they may gather in larger groups. Late in one year at least seventeen slept in two neighboring orange trees, eleven of them on the same low branch. In the half century that I have lived among these abundant birds, I have seen them fight only once. As I passed by the feeder on a February morning, downy feathers drifted earthward; beneath them two Golden-masked Tanagers lay locked together on the lawn. Soon they separated and flew off with two other adults, four in all.

More frequently than they fight, Golden-masks chase one another. One year, on many an evening from July to December when breeding was in abeyance, two pairs flew among the trees in our garden, mildly chasing one another and incessantly repeating their ticking notes. After these pursuits had continued for some fifteen to thirty minutes, the tanagers would fly off, two by two, in different directions. Similarly, at the approach of the nesting season, I have watched Common Bush-Tanagers chase one another, with brief grappling encounters. Probably, by such interactions, breeding pairs are spaced out. With the exception of Scarlet-rumped and Silver-beaked tanagers, I have not found two nests of the same species of tanagers close together.

Strangely, the most obvious and persistent contests for territory which I have noticed among tanagers were not by species permanently resident in the tropics but by migratory Summer Tanagers. After their arrival in Central America in late September or October, these visitors from the north claim individual territories that they will try to maintain until their departure the following March or April. Often the same attractive location is coveted by two of them—adult males in full red plumage, yellowish females or males in their first winter, or older males whose yellow plumage is becoming tinged with red. Young birds may compete with older ones, or males with females. From tree to tree they pursue one another, voicing soft, complaining notes; the *chicky-tucky-tuck* call; occasionally low, rattling notes; or snatches of subdued song. I have never seen them clash together. The dispute may continue for a full month, at the end of which their plumage looks too fresh to have been damaged by fighting. Sometimes a younger male, only tinged with red, retains possession of the preferred territory, while his all-red rival settles in an adjoining one.

Although it is rash to say of any bird that it *never* fights, tanagers certainly do so rarely. Mild-mannered fruit-eaters, they settle their differences by displaying, calling, chasing, and patience.

6 Temperament

A Gray Catbird in a northern garden and a Slaty Antshrike in a tropical forest have pecked the hand that I placed on their nests. Incubating antbirds have permitted me to photograph them while I stood, unconcealed, close beside them. A female Red-capped Manakin suffered me to pose her by hand on the nest for a picture. Anis and woodpeckers have struck me when I visited their nestlings. Although I have examined hundreds of tanagers' nests, I have never enjoyed such close contacts with any tanager. They are wary creatures, distrustful of man, perhaps because of direct persecution by aboriginal Americans and their European successors; moreover, as birds of tropical woodlands where monkeys abound, they have had a long ancestral experience with the grasping hands of primates. Nevertheless, I have sometimes set a ladder beneath the high nest of a euphonia or other small tanager, climbed up, and almost touched the sitting bird before she flew out.

For insight into the temperament of a bird, one must be closely associated with it for a long while, as I have been with the Scarlet-rumped Tanagers living around all the dwellings I have occupied in southern Costa Rica for half a century. I have found these tanagers consistently nervous, excitable, and suspicious. My earliest attempts to study them at the nest were frustrated by their distrust of a blind that most small birds, including forest dwellers, soon accept as a harmless addition to their surroundings. When I set a brown blind forty feet (12 m) from a nest of four-day-old nestlings, their mother abandoned it. After nesting for years in the shrubbery around our house, where they are never persecuted by people—although they have other enemies, such as snakes and squirrels—they have become much less timorous but not really trusting. One can rarely approach

White-shouldered Tanager
Tachyphonus luctuosus
Male perched on an orchid,
Maxillaria neglecta.
Honduras to Bolivia
and Amazonian Brazil.

within yards of an incubating or brooding female without caus-
ing her departure from the nest. None sat as tightly as the Western Tanager who permitted human hands to lift her from her
nest.

Incidents at the feeder reveal aspects of the temperament of
Scarlet-rumped Tanagers. Soon after I settled at "Los Cusingos,"
I began placing bananas each day on a board in a guava tree beside the house. The Scarlet-rumped Tanagers were the first birds
to find the food, and they have always been the feeder's most frequent attendants. When the chickens on the farm discovered
that they could fly up and eat the birds' fruit, I moved the board
to a higher site in a burío tree, about sixty feet (18 m) from its
original position. I had hardly descended from the ladder before
the tanagers, who had been watching me, flew into the burío
tree, calling sharply *ac* or *wac*, their usual note of excitement.
At first they looked down at the enticing fruit from a higher
bough, not daring to approach it. After five minutes a female descended to the board, bounced up like a rubber ball, dropped and
bounced again, and, after descending a third time, snatched a
hasty bite. Soon gaining confidence, she ate more freely. Another female, then a male, joined her at the feast. Before long,
birds of a dozen kinds, from honeycreepers to woodpeckers, were
coming in a steady stream.

When I replaced a stained, rotting board with bright new wood
in the same position, the tanagers were upset. I made the change
in midmorning. Through the remainder of the day they came
again and again to look down on the new board and cry out in
excitement or protest, without once, as far as I saw, daring to
alight on it. Meanwhile, less suspicious Buff-throated Saltators
and tanagers of four other species enjoyed the fruit, although attendance at the feeder was temporarily diminished. On the following morning, while a Speckled Tanager ate banana, a male
Scarlet-rumped Tanager looked down from above, then descended to the board, only to spring up as though it had burned
his feet. He dropped down and shot up again, then flew away
without having eaten. Presently, another male Scarlet-rumped
Tanager came and ate and was joined by a female. After this,
these birds visited the feeder repeatedly, in smaller numbers for
the next few days.

In a later year, when I replaced a rotting asphalt-coated feeder with a new one that differed chiefly in being a shinier black, Scarlet-rumped Tanagers behaved in much the same way. For two days they remained aloof, while Silver-throated Tanagers, Red-legged Honeycreepers, and other birds alighted on the glossy new board. The attendance of all the birds gradually increased during the following days. When, after many years, squirrels discovered this feeder and carried off the bananas, I began placing the fruit on the sill of a dining-room window, which was difficult for the rodents to reach. It did not take long for the birds to find it there. Soon male Scarlet-rumped Tanagers were eating freely, even while we sat at the table two yards away. In our absence, they would even enter through the open window and peck into bananas on the table. The more timid females did not come to the window until after the males had formed the habit. They have continued to be more shy, leaving abruptly if, while we are sitting at the table, we turn our heads to look directly at them. Males are not so often perturbed by our gaze; some have become, for Scarlet-rumped Tanagers, surprisingly confident.

When something strange excites Scarlet-rumped Tanagers, their cries of alarm or protest advise all the avian community. During the Costa Rican revolution of 1948, mercenary troops hired by the tottering government wandered through the Valley of El General, killing, burning, and plundering. Although, fortunately, they never reached our farm, repeated rumors that they were coming our way caused us to tie up the horses in the densest thickets and hurriedly hide as many of our more valuable possessions as we could. On one of these occasions, I threw a pair of new shoes into dense shrubbery as the quickest way of concealing them. Before long, the excited cries of a crowd of Scarlet-rumped Tanagers drew me to the shrubbery, where I expected to find nothing less than a big snake. The only thing out of the ordinary that I could detect there was my pair of new shoes!

Usually a commotion among the tanagers in the garden does reveal the presence of a snake. Occasionally, however, it is incited by nothing more formidable than an exceptionally large moth, perhaps tattered and moribund after torrential rains the preceding afternoon and night, slowly waving its wide, dark wings while it dies. The cries of the Scarlet-rumped Tanagers draw tanagers of other kinds, as well as finches, wood-warblers, wrens, flycatchers, hummingbirds, sometimes an antbird from the neighboring forest, until the poor moth is surrounded by a motley feathered crowd, flitting around and complaining in a typical mobbing party. None touches the sluggish insect, which from time to time moves its wings more widely, arousing a fresh spasm of excitement among the birds. After a while the birds drift away, leaving the moth to expire in peace, but if a passing Scarlet-rumped Tanager notices it again, its loud calls may attract another group of mobbers. This is strange behavior for birds that must be familiar with the abundant large, harmless moths of the tropics; but let us try to imagine how we might react to an insect as big as ourselves. And it is hardly surprising in a bird that will mob a pair of shoes.

On the lawn beneath a spreading mango tree one April afternoon, I watched a female Scarlet-rumped Tanager approach a praying mantis. The green insect reared up on its middle legs and hindlegs, holding its forelegs—separated from the others by nearly the whole length of its long, thin thorax—somewhat elevated and widely spread. At the same time, it extended sideward its short, broad green forewings, revealing on each a nearly round, dull red spot with an elongated black mark at the center and yellow at its edge, the whole forming a crude eyespot. The transparent, mostly colorless pleated hindwings were boldly painted with narrow, transverse yellow bands. In menacing attitude, displaying these strikingly colored wings, the mantis confronted the tanager, waving its forelegs toward her. Uttering notes of excitement or alarm, the bird advanced close to the insect but did not appear to touch it. Presently she flew away but soon returned, to be greeted by the same threatening forelegs. With another cry, the tanager again retreated. I picked up the uninjured mantis. It was nearly 2.5 inches (6 cm) long, and its forewings measured 1.25 inches (3 cm) long by nearly 0.5 inch (1.3 cm) broad. It might have made a substantial meal for a bird bold enough to seize it.

On another occasion, I saw a large green longhorn grasshopper, or locust, fly across a pasture, closely pursued by a male and a female Scarlet-rumped Tanager. The insect alighted in low herbage; the birds continued beyond it, but soon the male tanager returned to the orthopteron, which had climbed up a foot-high (30 cm) sprout. Whenever the bird started to attack, the insect spread its dark brown, green-margined underwings and violently shook both itself and its support. After a few feints of attack, the bird withdrew, leaving the insect unharmed. The grasshopper behaved the same way when I touched it. These episodes reveal not only the value of the markings and ruses by which apparently palatable insects save themselves from being devoured but also an inconsistency in the temperament of Scarlet-rumped Tanagers. As chapter 11 details, they boldly attack snakes that menace them and their nests yet are too timid to make a meal of an insect that compensates for lack of effective defense by bluffing. However, it is not surprising that they take greater risks to protect their progeny than to capture an insect when other foods are readily available.

Plate 1. Tawny-bellied Euphonia
Euphonia imitans
Male (above left; 4 in., 10 cm) and female
(above right; same size). Southern Pacific
Costa Rica and western Pacific Panama.

Green Honeycreeper *Chlorophanes spiza*
(below left)
Male (5.5 in., 14 cm). Southeastern Mexico
to southern Brazil.

Spectacled Owl *Pulsatrix perspicillata*
(below right)
Sexes similar (18 in., 46 cm). Southern
Mexico to northern Argentina.

Plate 2. Grass-green Tanager
Chlorornis riefferii
Sexes alike (8.5 in., 21.5 cm). Andes
from Colombia to Bolivia.

Plate 3. Black-and-yellow Tanager
Chrysothlypis chrysomelas
Male (5 in., 12.5 cm). Costa Rica to eastern Panama.

Plate 4. Guira Tanager *Hemithraupis guira*
Male (5.25 in., 13.5 cm). Tropical South America.

Plate 5. Western Tanager *Piranga ludoviciana*
Male (7 in., 18 cm). Southeastern Alaska to northern Baja California;
winters as far south as Costa Rica.

Plate 6. Silver-throated Tanager *Tangara icterocephala*
Sexes similar (5.25 in., 13.5 cm). Costa Rica to northwestern Ecuador.

Plate 7. Scarlet Tanager *Piranga olivacea*
Female (above; 7 in., 18 cm) and male (below;
same size). Southern Canada and eastern and
central United States; winters from Panama
to northwestern Bolivia.

Plate 8. Speckled Tanager *Tangara guttata*
Sexes similar (5.25 in., 13.5 cm). Costa Rica to Venezuela
and northern Brazil.

Plate 9. Golden-browed Chlorophonia *Chlorophonia callophrys*
Male (above; 5.25 in., 13.5 cm) and female (below; same size).
Costa Rica and western Panama.

Plate 10. Golden-masked Tanager *Tangara larvata*
Adults (above; sexes alike; 5 in., 12.5 cm) and immature (feeding nestling). Southeastern Mexico to western Ecuador.

Plate 11. Burnished-buff Tanager
Tangara cayana
Male (above; 5.5 in., 14 cm) and female (below;
same size). Tropical South America.

Plate 12. Gray-headed Tanager
Eucometis penicillata
Sexes alike (6.75 in., 17 cm). Southeastern Mexico
to southern Brazil.

Plate 13. Scarlet-thighed Dacnis *Dacnis venusta*
Male (4.5 in., 11.5 cm). Costa Rica to
northwestern Ecuador.

Plate 14. (facing page) Red-crowned Ant-Tanager
Habia rubica
Male (above; 7 in., 18 cm) and female (below; same size).
Central Mexico to northeastern Argentina.

Plate 15. Scarlet-rumped Tanager *Ramphocelus passerinii*
Male (above; 6.25 in., 16 cm) and female (below; same size).
Southeastern Mexico to western Panama.

Plate 16. Paradise Tanager *Tangara chilensis*
Sexes alike (6 in., 15 cm). Northern South America to Amazonia.

Plate 17. Crimson-collared Tanager *Ramphocelus sanguinolentus*
Sexes alike (6.5 in., 16.5 cm). Southeastern Mexico to central Panama.

Plate 18. Tawny-capped Euphonia *Euphonia anneae*
Male (4.25 in., 11 cm). Costa Rica to northwestern Colombia.

Plate 19. (facing page) Rosy Thrush-Tanager *Rhodinocichla rosea*
Male (7.75 in., 19.5 cm). Western Mexico; Costa Rica to northern
South America.

Plate 20. Multicolored Tanager *Chlorochrysa nitidissima*
Male (5 in., 12.5 cm). Female similar but duller. Colombia.

Plate 21. (facing page) Magpie-Tanager
Cissopis leveriana
Sexes alike (11 in., 28 cm). Northern South America
to southeastern Brazil.

Plate 22. White-throated Shrike-Tanager
Lanio leucothorax
Male (7.5 in., 19 cm). Honduras to western
Panama.

Plate 23. Hooded Mountain-Tanager *Buthraupis montana*
Sexes alike (8.5 in., 21.5 cm). Colombia and Venezuela to Bolivia.

Plate 24. (following page) Scarlet-and-white Tanager
Erythrothlypis salmoni
Male (5 in., 12.5 cm). Western Colombia to northwestern Ecuador.

7 Courtship and Nests

In tropical regions with a definite dry season, tanagers, like many other birds, prepare to breed when the rains return. Among birds that are permanently resident and, often, continuously mated, the acquisition of territory and the formation of pairs is rarely so conspicuous and exciting as it is among migratory birds who hurriedly arrange these matters as they settle into a new life after their return from their winter homes. A male and female who have long been intimately associated need no elaborate displays to attune themselves for reproduction. At the approach of the nesting season, male tanagers of many species feed their mates more frequently. At the feeder, I have watched Golden-masked, Speckled, Silver-throated, Blue-gray, and Palm tanagers solemnly pass billfuls of banana to mates busily helping themselves to the same fruit. Elsewhere, I have seen males of the Green Honeycreeper, Blue Dacnis, Golden-browed Chlorophonia, and Tawny-bellied Euphonia feed their partners. Sometimes the female Tawny-bellied Euphonia returns the courtesy.

Among the highly migratory Scarlet Tanagers, a male establishes a territory and courts a female by more conspicuous behavior than has been recorded for tropical members of the family. Arriving in the northeastern United States from South America in spring, he advertises his choice of territory by singing almost continuously, high in burgeoning trees whose young foliage hardly conceals his brilliant figure. Frequently he engages in a loud "song duel" with a neighboring male or, approaching closer to his rival, displays threateningly until he chases the other back to his own area. Appearing a few days later, a female is attracted by his singing. When she enters his territory, he stops his loud treetop caroling to follow her while she forages among lower boughs, at intervals singing softly and briefly when near her. Occasionally the two call to each other with a high-pitched *sweeeeeee, sweeeeeee, sweeeeeeet.*

In an open space in the woods, the male Scarlet Tanager descends to leafless branches or shrubs rarely as much as two yards (2 m) high, sometimes almost to the ground, where he slightly spreads and depresses his wings, fully exposing his upper plumage. The female, peering down from a perch well above him, views an elongated patch of scarlet bordered by the black wings and tail. As the male traces a circular course through the open space, flying always near the ground, the female follows at a higher level, alighting above him and looking down whenever he perches on a dead twig to repeat his display.

With the exception of euphonias and chlorophonias, all tanagers whose nests are known build open cups, though they differ greatly in situation, size, and materials. Usually they are placed amid the foliage of a tree or shrub or in the mossy crotch of a tree; rarely, they are on the ground. Species of *Piranga*, including the Scarlet, Summer, Western, and Flame-colored tanagers, usually build at midheight of the trees; exceptional nests are as high as seventy-five feet (23 m) or as low as four feet (1.2 m) above the ground. Common Bush-Tanagers nest among epiphytes on high boughs of montane trees or at ground level in pastures.

Blue-gray Tanagers choose an even wider variety of sites, from a hundred feet (30 m) up in a tree to, exceptionally, on the ground amid concealing sprouts. Even a beam in an open shed may support their open cup. Like other small tanagers, they sometimes hide their nests between the upturned green "fingers" of a bunch of bananas on the plant—a deceptively alluring site. As the hard green bananas grow fatter, they may so reduce the width of the space through which the Blue-grays enter and leave their nest that the birds are unable to reach and feed their nestlings—unless (as must happen rarely) some human friend comes to their aid and enlarges the opening. Or the green bunch may be harvested, to ripen in the grower's house or to be shipped abroad, by someone who is unaware that a nest is concealed inside and would likely not spare it even if he noticed. Or the bananas may ripen before the nestlings can fly, attracting a variety of mammals that would welcome this addition to their fare.

Instead of building a nest for themselves, versatile Blue-gray Tanagers may appropriate that of some other bird. Once, when a pair of these tanagers and a pair of Boat-billed Flycatchers, who were nesting in neighboring trees, both lost their eggs to a predator, the tanagers promptly took possession of the structure of the much bigger flycatchers, reduced the size of the bowl with a thick lining, and laid their eggs in it. Another pair of Blue-gray Tanagers remodeled the nest of a slightly larger Scarlet-rumped Tanager and raised a family there. In Venezuela I saw Blue-gray Tanagers occupying rooms in nests with several chambers, built with interlaced twigs by Rufous-fronted Thornbirds, one pair of tanagers in each of the thornbirds' hanging structures. The thornbirds still occupied these nests, sleeping or breeding in rooms above the one claimed by the interlopers. On the llanos of Venezuela, I also watched a Glaucous Tanager carry material into the unfinished nest of Rufous-fronted Thornbirds.

Sometimes Blue-gray Tanagers capture a small nest containing eggs of the builders. Twice I have known them to displace Golden-masked Tanagers and incubate the eggs of both species. In one of these stolen nests they hatched a Golden-masked nestling and reared it, along with their own two young, until it flew. However, it apparently died, presumably because its calls did not attract the foster parents, whose own progeny remained in the nest several days longer. The other nest with a mixed set of eggs was destroyed by a predator.

The related Palm Tanagers more consistently choose an enclosed site for their nests. Perhaps most frequently their choice is a nook among the broad bases of the enormous fronds of a tall palm tree, where the nest is invisible from the ground. Or they build in a cavity high in a trunk, in a cranny beneath a house roof, on a porch beam, in the open end of a tubular rainspout, or in a compact mass of epiphytes. Golden-masked Tanagers usually nest in the foliage of trees. On rare occasions, however, they may occupy an old woodpecker's hole or other cavity high in a tree; a long, swinging pouch woven and abandoned by an oropendola; or the interior of a bunch of green bananas.

Other tanagers consistently build their nests lower. In the undergrowth of the forest the favorite site of Gray-headed Tanagers is the crown of a small palm, bristling with long, sharp black

Black-faced Tanager *Schistochlamys melanopis*
Male. Tropical South America.

spines. Like a number of other rain-forest birds, these tanagers often emerge from the tall woodland to nest in neighboring gardens, plantations, or other clearings, where predation is reduced and the chances of a successful nesting are somewhat greater. (The reverse of this tendency—birds of open or semi-open country entering closed forest to breed—is much rarer.) When the Gray-headed Tanagers temporarily leave the forest to nest, they build in orange trees, coffee shrubs, or hedges; but wherever they nest, their sites are rarely more than seven feet (2 m) above the ground. Another tanager that prefers low sites is the Scarlet-rumped, whose nests in plantations, gardens, and thickets are mostly from four to twelve feet (1.2–3.7 m) up, rarely as low as one foot (30 cm) or as high as twenty feet (6 m).

Euphonias and chlorophonias build globular nests with a side entrance, which require support at the sides as well as below. The euphonias that dwell in humid forests, including the Olive-backed and the Tawny-bellied, often tuck their nests into a pocket in the mosses, liverworts, and larger epiphytes that thickly cover upright trunks. A pair of Tawny-bellied Euphonias sometimes choose a stout segment of a dead branch, laden with such aerial growths, which has broken away from the base of the limb and hangs below it, attached only by the root of an epi-phyte and swaying in every breeze. Dangling masses of epiphytic roots also support nests of this species and of White-vented Euphonias. In the mountains of Mexico, Blue-hooded Euphonias hide their nests in long, pendent gray skeins of Spanish moss (the epiphytic bromeliad *Tillandsia usneoides*).

In open country, euphonias choose a variety of sites, usually different from those in forests. A cranny in the top of a decaying fence post or a shallow cavity high or low in a tree, especially if screened by epiphytes, often shelters a nest. A nook in the matted roots of orchids growing on posts or in a wire basket hanging near a house is an acceptable site. When a more sheltered situation is not available, euphonias may build amid the close-set, upright twigs of a tree or between the shoots that sprout thickly around the truncated top of a living fence post. One pair of Yellow-crowned Euphonias tucked their nest into the folds of a large dead leaf of a cecropia tree which had lodged in the crown of a banana plant. Violaceous Euphonias often build their nests

at the tops of banks beside paths, and Yellow-throated Euphonias sometimes breed in streamside or roadside banks, in holes
that they probably did not dig themselves.

Occasionally, like other tanagers, euphonias occupy a nest
that they did not build. A pair of Thick-billed Euphonias carried
material into the bulky, domed nest of a Great Kiskadee Flycatcher, which rested atop a pendent many-chambered nest of
Rufous-fronted Thornbirds. Yellow-throated Euphonias occupied
the long, slender nest, with a shallow niche in its midst, that a
Royal Flycatcher had suspended from a liana over a forest stream
in Belize. Yellow-crowned Euphonias built between the layered
brood cells of an old, dilapidated wasp's nest at the top of a tall
fig tree, but apparently the birds did not incubate eggs in this
vespiary.

The nests even of birds in the same genus may vary greatly in
composition. In the open cup (bulky for so small a bird) of the
Silver-throated Tanager, the foundation and outer wall are composed of a great mass of green mosses and liverworts with a few
pieces of small-leaved ferns, such as diminutive polypodies, and
sometimes dry, branching inflorescences. The shallow or deep
hollow in this massive cup is lined with dry leaves, including
nearly whole small leaves of dicotyledonous trees, strips torn
from great monocotyledonous leaves such as those of wild plan-
tains and shellflowers, and blades of grasses. A thin mat of
coarse fibers and "vegetable horsehair" (thin fungal rhizomorphs
that creep over decaying branches in humid forests) covers the
bottom, where the eggs lie.

The related Speckled Tanager, a bird of about the same size,
builds a smaller, more compact nest, with little or no green material. The exterior is composed largely of slender, curved, spiny
secondary rachises of the bipinnate leaves of a species of *Mimosa*, mixed with a few wiry rootlets and tendrils. Small, partly
decayed leaves of dicotyledonous plants or long strips of banana
leaves are placed among the rachises, becoming more abundant
toward the inside. Interbedded with these materials and holding
them together are long fungal filaments or true horsehairs. A
mat of these black fibrous materials, with gray foliaceous lichens loosely placed, makes a bed for the eggs. Cobweb, that in-

dispensable binder of small birds' nests, helps fasten this cup to supporting twigs.

The larger Scarlet-rumped Tanager builds a substantial open cup, four to five inches (10–12.5 cm) in overall diameter by two and a half to three inches (6.5–7.5 cm) in height. The bulk of the nest usually consists of dry leaves, often strips from the foliage of the banana or related monocotyledonous plants, which may be two to three inches (5–7.5 cm) broad; if such leaves are not available, the narrower blades of grasses are used. These flat pieces are held together by an outer network of coarse, fibrous materials—thin, dry herbaceous vines, wiry roots, weed stems, fungal rhizomorphs, horsehairs, bast fibers, or the like. More of these strands are placed between the layers of leaves; others are coiled down in the bottom to form a thin lining on which the eggs rest. Often the outside is decorated with a spray or two of living ferns, such as the small-leaved, wiry-stemmed *Polypodium ciliatum* that creeps over trunks and branches in rainy regions, or pieces of the larger fronds of some other fern. Rarely, a Scarlet-rumped Tanager adds to her nest many billfuls of soft seed down from the balsa tree or some other source.

Dusky-faced Tanagers are so different in many ways from other members of the family that it is not surprising that they build a very different nest. After much searching, I found the only known nest of this large tanager, a bulky open cup slung between two thin, upright branches, a few inches apart, in a tangled riverside thicket. Unlike most other tanagers' nests that I have seen, the bottom was not supported. This nest was composed almost wholly of the long, brown, threadlike pistillate inflorescences of the small tree *Myriocarpa*, some of which were wrapped around the supporting branches and many more spread untidily over surrounding leaves and twigs, especially beneath the nest. Mixed with the inflorescences were a few thin rootlets and pieces of an epiphytic fern with small, entire, living leaves. Black filaments of vegetable horsehair made the sparse lining.

Different again from the nests of other tanagers is that of another atypical species, the Rosy Thrush-Tanager. The only nest I have seen was situated a yard (1 m) above the ground in a tangle of bushes and vines in a low, dense thicket. It consisted of a foundation of coarse twigs supporting a shallow bowl made of secondary rachises of the twice-compound leaves of the acacia-like *Calliandra similis*. It resembled the nests of certain mockingbirds and thrashers more than a tanager's nest.

Honeycreepers' nests are diverse. A nest of the Shining Honeycreeper was a shallow cup attached by its rim to high, thin horizontal twigs of a tall timber bamboo, beneath a small wasp's nest. In form it resembled the nest of a vireo or a manakin but was a slighter structure, composed of slender, dark strands so thinly applied that I could count the eggs through the bottom. Although such a nest provides poor insulation for the eggs and young, it has the advantage of drying rather quickly after one of the frequent tropical showers. The Red-legged Honeycreeper's nest is similar but more substantial, composed of more varied materials.

A nest of the Scarlet-thighed Dacnis was a slight, frail, open bowl, scarcely more than a hammock, so shallow that I marveled that it could retain eggs in the wind-tossed crown of a tree. The underside of the thin fabric was completely covered with green living pieces of the fern *Nephrolepis pendula*, some of which were four inches (10 cm) long. This nest was exceedingly hard to find, even after the movements of the parents and the calls of hungry nestlings revealed its approximate location in a tangle of green parasitic vines amid high leafy boughs. In contrast to the nests of the other honeycreepers, the Green Honeycreeper's shallow, open cup, about three inches (7.5 cm) broad and two inches (5 cm) high, is composed mainly of whole, small, dead dicotyledonous leaves held together by fine, tough fungal filaments, dry inflorescence stalks, tendrils, cobweb, and thin, curved, minutely spiny secondary rachises of the twice-compound leaves of the climbing mimosa.

The little globes that euphonias build in crannies of posts or trees or in pockets in the moss that covers their trunks are three to four inches (7.5–10 cm) in diameter. The round doorway in the side measures about an inch and a half (3.8 cm). The outside is often green with mosses, liverworts, living filmy ferns, or other minature ferns. Other materials used are fibrous roots of epiphytes, light-colored plant fibers, black vegetable horsehair, seed plumes, strips of bark, grass blades, shriveled small leaves, fluffy tufts of white cotton (where available), and often much cobweb to bind everything together. In the highlands, chlorophonias pull green moss and fibrous rootlets from high trunks and boughs to build their nests, which in form are much like those of euphonias, amid mosses and other epiphytes high in trees, where they are difficult to detect unless one sees the parents approach them.

The nest site is probably selected by both members of a pair as inseparable as mated Golden-masked, Speckled, and Blue-gray tanagers. If only the female builds the nest, she alone appears to choose the location; but this is not invariable. Although the female Scarlet-rumped Tanager constructs her nest unassisted, she and her mate together sometimes prospect for a site. The more attentive males take great interest in their partner's activities and appear to influence the female's choice of a place to build. Early one April a male repeatedly came alone to sing in a shrub of *Thunbergia erecta* in front of my study window. After this had continued for several days, his mate arrived to rest at intervals in the same place, among close-set twigs near the top of the bush, usually while her partner perched, often singing, below her. On the day following her visits, the female started to build at the site that she had repeatedly tested, in the shrub that her mate preferred for the nest.

Only females of the following species have been seen building: Scarlet-rumped, Crimson-backed, and Crimson-collared tanagers (*Ramphocelus*); Red-crowned and Red-throated ant-tanagers (*Habia*); Scarlet and Flame-colored tanagers (*Piranga*); Common Bush-Tanagers (*Chlorospingus*); Red-legged and Shining honeycreepers (*Cyanerpes*); Blue Dacnis (*Dacnis*); and Green Honeycreepers (*Chlorophanes*). A male who does not build often follows his partner back and forth while she gathers materials for the nest, or he may sing or call nearby while the female shapes the structure. From time to time some of these males pick up and toy with materials, only to drop them instead of adding them to the incipient nest. Female Bay-headed and Silver-throated tanagers (*Tangara*) commonly receive only occasional or token help from their mate. Both sexes of the following species take substantial part in building: Blue-gray, Palm, and Yellow-winged tanagers (*Thraupis*); Gray-headed Tanagers (*Eucometis*); and Golden-masked and Speckled tanagers (*Tangara*). I have watched the construction of one or more nests of seven species of euphonias and several nests of Golden-browed Chlorophonias, and I have never failed to see both sexes take fairly equal shares in the undertaking. Sometimes the male brings materials more frequently, sometimes the female.

In northern woods, female Scarlet Tanagers gather most of their materials from the ground. Occasionally they try to break a twig from a fallen branch or even a living tree, not always with success. In the tropics, abundant aerial growths are a fertile source of materials for tanagers and other birds, who often tug strenuously to detach a root of an epiphyte while clinging to it or hovering on wing. Usually they gather several pieces in their bill before flying back to the nest.

A pair of Gray-headed Tanagers actively building is a delight to watch. They are rather noisy, calling much, the male singing sweetly while he carries a billful of materials or sits in the nest, shaping it. The partners come and go separately rather than together. When one, arriving with a contribution, finds the other sitting in the nest, it may pass its billful to its mate; but often it prefers to add its materials directly to the structure. Sometimes the tanager arriving with fibers and finding the nest occupied is so impatient to deposit its load that it alights on the other's back, making the latter rise and fly away. The swift departure shakes off the bird on top, but it soon returns to deposit its billful and arrange it in the growing structure.

More often, when both sexes build actively, they come and go together, as is the way of Golden-masked Tanagers, Blue-gray Tanagers, euphonias, and chlorophonias. When one of the pair arrives without material, it may be because it had not yet found anything suitable when the other, already with a full bill, was starting toward the nest. Rather than be left behind, the slower partner accompanies the other, with empty bill. Euphonias prefer to add directly to the nest whatever they bring, instead of passing it to the partner already inside. At some nests either sex may enter first; at others the male nearly always does so, thereby establishing an order that will be consistently followed in feeding the nestlings. While one arranges its contribution, the other perches nearby, to enter as soon as the former emerges. Then this bird waits, sometimes finding on a neighboring branch a tuft of moss that it carries into the nest after its partner exits. When both are ready, they fly away together.

In addition to contributing to the construction of the nest, some male tanagers—including the Golden-masked, Speckled, and Silver-throated—give food to their partners while they build. In five and a half hours of watching, I saw a male Silver-throat bring material to the nest only five times, while the female did so 115 times, but he fed her six times. Probably he gave her more food while the two were out of sight, as males often pass billfuls to their partners at the feeder and elsewhere. One male Silver-throat tried to feed his mate as she approached the nest with a big piece of leaf. Finding that with so full a bill she could not take the proffered food, he followed her to the nest and fed her after she had deposited her burden. While another female Silver-throat was away from the nest she was building in a gardenia, her partner flew into the shrub with food in his bill. Soon the female arrived with a piece of fruit, apparently guava, too big to swallow. After clearing his mouth, the male took it from her, worked on it for a while, part of the time on the ground, reduced it to swallowable size, and returned it to his mate, who promptly ate it. Then both flew away together. The male Silver-throat who built most actively was not seen to feed his co-worker.

Building tanagers use procedures widespread among passerines and other small birds: tucking in materials with the bill, arranging them with bill and feet, shaping the bowl against the breast with vigorous movements of the body. Many tanagers take from three to six days to build a nest, although construction is sometimes prolonged to a week or two, especially at nests begun very early in the season, before conditions for breeding are optimum. In the north a Scarlet Tanager has been reported to complete her nest in one day, although more often a female takes from three to six days, as do tropical members of the family. Not infrequently, a female tanager lays her first egg on the morning following the day she finishes her nest; more often, the nest remains empty for one to three or four days before the first egg appears. The whole interval between the beginning of building and the start of laying is frequently four to seven days; occasionally it is much longer.

8 Eggs and Incubation

In the tropics tanagers lay their eggs early in the morning, from before to soon after sunrise, on consecutive days. In the inner tropics, between about twelve degrees north and twelve degrees south latitude, by far the most frequent number of eggs is two; sets of one or three are much less common. Some sets of three or more are probably the product of two females laying in the same nest. When only a single egg is present, the other may have been lost before the nest was examined. As with many other birds, clutch size increases with distance from the equator, the so-called latitude effect. In Belize, at seventeen degrees north latitude, Red-throated and Red-crowned ant-tanagers commonly lay three eggs, although nearer the equator, as in Costa Rica and Trinidad, the latter nearly always lays two. In the United States, Summer, Scarlet, and Western tanagers lay three to five eggs, most often four. In northern Argentina, well south of the Tropic of Capricorn, three or four eggs are commonly found in tanagers' nests. The foregoing statements do not apply to euphonias, which hardly range beyond the tropics and even in the inner tropics usually lay three or four, and sometimes five, of their tiny eggs.

Tanagers' eggs are bright blue, blue-green, blue-gray, greenish, cream, pinkish white, or white, spotted, blotched, or scrawled with shades of brown or lilac, or from sparingly to thickly with black. Usually scattered over the whole surface, these markings become concentrated in a wreath or cap on the thicker end, where they may almost conceal the ground color. Eggs in the same set may differ in density of pigmentation.

Although the male Rosy Thrush-Tanager has been reported to share incubation with his mate, in some twenty-three other species in twelve genera that have been carefully watched—including the larger tanagers, honeycreepers, euphonias, and chlorophonias—only the female has been found sitting on the eggs. Usually she begins to incubate on the day she lays her last egg. The amount of time she spends incubating may increase during the next day or two, after which it remains about the same until the eggs hatch. There is no marked increase in the last few days, but usually minor fluctuations occur from day to day, caused by changes in the weather, perhaps by her success in finding food, or by other factors more obscure.

The length of the female's incubation sessions varies greatly with the species and the individual; the sessions may last only a few minutes, and they rarely exceed an hour. Often they fall within the range of twenty to thirty-five minutes, about the time it takes a small bird to digest a berry, but they may be much longer. The intervals of sitting by a Tawny-bellied Euphonia varied from one hour and seventeen minutes to one hour and forty-eight minutes and averaged one hour and twenty-seven minutes. Once I watched a Bay-headed Tanager incubate continuously for two hours and fourteen minutes in clear weather. Rain often keeps birds covering their nests longer than they do on clear days. During a prolonged afternoon rain a tiny Red-legged Honeycreeper sat for three hours, continuously except for an interruption of three minutes when she was frightened from the nest by a passing man. On two rainy afternoons a little Shining Honeycreeper sat continuously for four hours the first day and for six and a half hours the second.

Intervals of sitting alternate with recesses, or intermissions, which tend to be longer when they follow a long period of motionless sitting without much food coming from the mate but which nearly always are much shorter on average than the sessions. In an active day of usually about ten to twelve hours, counting from the female's first morning departure from her nest to her final return for the night (which sometimes occurs well before sunset), most tanagers keep their eggs covered from 60 to 80 percent of the time, which is the range of constancy of many other incubating passerine birds.

Table 1 shows in more detail how incubating tanagers of ten species pass their days. Except for the Crimson-backed Tanager I watched in Panama and the Scarlet Tanagers that Kenneth W. Prescott studied in Michigan, all the observations were made in

Table 1. Incubation patterns of female tanagers

Species	Hours of record	Number[1]	Sessions (min.) Range	Sessions (min.) Average	Recesses (min.) Range	Recesses (min.) Average	Constancy (%)
Speckled Tanager	12.5	14	30–53	39.7	2–27	10.1	80
Speckled Tanager	12.5	14	20–77	37.8	3–23	11.4	77
Golden-masked Tanager	10	20	2–47	22.6	2–11	7.3	76
Blue Dacnis	12	20	11–55	23.6	6–18	11.7	66
Green Honeycreeper	10	8	32–149	54.9	6–20	12.2	82
Shining Honeycreeper	12.75	9	14–390	69.0	7–23	14.3	81
Shining Honeycreeper	12.75	10	6–242	46.5	7–34	18.3	70
Tawny-bellied Euphonia	11.5	5	77–108	86.8	13–43	29.8	74
White-vented Euphonia	12.5	17	7–38	25.1	6–22	13.4	65
White-vented Euphonia	13	16	12–53	30.2	4–26	12.5	69
Scarlet-rumped Tanager	12	16	8–102+	29.3+	5–32	11.8	71+
Scarlet-rumped Tanager	12	15	12–104+	34.0+	7–19	11.9	74+
Crimson-backed Tanager	10	10	16–89	39.0	11–36	21.9	64
Scarlet Tanager (composite)	114.5	267	1–72	19.5	1–41	5.8	77

1. This column gives the number of sessions; the number of recesses may differ by one.

Costa Rica. Each line summarizes the record kept at one nest from dawn to dusk on one day or on the forenoon of one day and the afternoon of another day, usually the next; hence each record covers all hours of activity. Often the tanagers would end their long nocturnal session many minutes after I started to watch in the dawn and would return from the day's last outing to settle on the nest for the night while much daylight remained. The result was that the total time of the sessions plus the total time of the recesses was less than the length of the watch. Since the incubating bird's day begins and ends with an outing, it contains one more recess than it does sessions. I calculated constancy by dividing the average length of the sessions by the average length of sessions plus the average length of recesses and multiplying the quotient by 100. Unlike all the other records, that for the Scarlet Tanager is a composite based on thirty-four watches, each lasting from one to seven hours, at ten nests. These northern tanagers incubated with about the same constancy as the tropical species.

When an incubating tanager returns from an outing, she is often accompanied by her mate to a spot near the nest, but there is great variability in the attentiveness of male tanagers at this stage of the nesting. Male euphonias and chlorophonias are outstandingly attentive. After the pair return together and alight in front of their nest with a side entrance, the female's entry is the occasion of a spectacular performance, widespread among these small birds. As she darts toward the doorway, her partner accompanies her so closely that he appears to try to reach it first. She always wins the race, while he veers to one side and flies afar, or, rarely, alights briefly on the nest's roof. Meanwhile, she shoots in and turns around in what appears to be one swiftly continuous movement. Whether incubating or brooding nestlings, she always sits with her head in the doorway, facing outward.

A female euphonia leaving a high nest, whether spontaneously or when disturbed, commonly seems to fall straight downward. Just before she strikes the ground, she curves sharply upward and rises into the branches of a tree. This ruse might deceive a predator that has not yet discovered a nest within its field of vision: unless the euphonia's flight is very closely watched, it appears to start at the point where she turns upward, well below the nest. By contrast, the race of a male and female toward the nest seems to be needlessly revealing. However, they probably would not approach it if either of the two pairs of sharp eyes detected a lurking enemy.

Believing that birds cannot distinguish between one and two, some bird-watchers walk with a companion to a blind before a nest that they intend to study; while one enters, the other ostentatiously marches away, presumably deceiving the sitting bird into believing that both bipeds have gone. If predators are so obtuse, the flight of two birds toward a nest from which one immediately flies away might confound them, too. Be this as it may, I believe the race to the nest is simply a manifestation of the euphonias' strong habit of flying with their partners, rather than a ruse to mislead predators. The falling departure from a high nest is frequent among small birds of other families; and the race to an enclosed nest, or one in a protected nook, is practiced by birds as different as tody-flycatchers, Bright-rumped Attilas, and Black-faced Grosbeaks.

As they settle down to incubate, tanagers, like most other birds, spread their abdominal feathers to bring the thick, warm bare skin of their incubation patch, richly supplied with blood vessels, into direct contact with their eggs. From time to time they rise to look down into the nest and adjust the eggs with their bills. Occasionally they preen their feathers. Beginning around midday and continuing into the early afternoon, Scarlet-rumped Tanagers take a "siesta," often sitting quietly in the nests for well over an hour, although their incubation sessions through the rest of the day rarely continue so long. They appear not to close their eyes or sleep at this time, the warmest part of the day, when their usually active companions also rest inconspicuously amid foliage. Greatly prolonged midday sessions have not been recorded of other tanagers.

Among incubating females that are fed on or near their nests by their mates are the Scarlet, Blue-gray, Golden-masked, Silver-throated, and Speckled tanagers, the Green Honeycreeper, Blue Dacnis, White-vented Euphonia, and Golden-browed Chlorophonia. As one pair of White-vented Euphonias approached their nest, the male begged with open bill and his mate regurgitated food to him—an unusual occurrence. One male Speckled Tanager fed his incubating mate ten times in a day, much more frequently than did males of the other species, whose visits to the nest were widely spaced. However, they probably fed their partners more often while the two foraged together beyond view of the watcher.

Male Scarlet-rumped Tanagers escort their mates to the nest on a minority of their returns to it but have not been seen to feed them. They bring food to the nest more often in the female's absence than while she is present. If she happens to be sitting on the eggs, she does not take it. Alighting on the nest's rim while the female is elsewhere, the male Scarlet-rumped Tanager lowers his head into the nest and appears to offer the morsel in his bill to the unhatched eggs. Similarly, a male of the related Crimson-backed Tanager brought insects to the nest while his mate was absent, bent his head down over the eggs, and murmured in a low, pleasant twitter, as though coaxing recently hatched nestlings to take food. When he arrived with a green insect while the female was incubating, he seemed as reluctant to give it to her as she was to receive it. Finally, she took it, only to return it to him. After further hesitation, she swallowed the offering, which appeared not to be intended for her.

Flame-faced Tanager
Tangara parzudakii
Sexes alike. Venezuela;
Colombia to Peru.

These male tanagers seemed impatient to feed their offspring days before they hatched. Such anticipatory food-bringing, by males more often than by females, has been witnessed in a number of species of diverse families. It makes me wonder what is passing in the minds of these birds that appear to be eagerly awaiting the birth of their progeny. Do they foresee the nestlings long before the eggs hatch?

Tanagers sometimes behave abnormally. For at least two weeks, a female Gray-headed Tanager "incubated" in an empty nest. Whether she had lost eggs before I found her or had never laid any, I could not learn. At night she slept in the eggless nest, and by day she sat in it, in the pattern of a Gray-headed Tanager incubating normally though with slightly reduced constancy. A mate accompanied her on her outings. Persistent sitting in empty nests is all too common among broody domestic hens who should be laying eggs for their owners, but it is rare among wild birds. One of the few reported cases involved the Takahe of New Zealand. A pair of these big rails took turns on an eggless nest for seven or eight weeks.

Departures from the strict monogamy prevalent in the tanager family have been observed only rarely. A small minority of female Scarlet-rumped Tanagers nesting with no attendant male seems to occur in seasons when females so outnumber males that not all can obtain mates. These solitary females associate with a mated male long enough to have their eggs fertilized, then rear their families alone. Similarly, when two females of the related Silver-beaked Tanagers nested three feet (90 cm) apart in the same shrub, no male was ever seen to attend either nest. Probably these tanagers are never truly polygamous, for this term implies an association of an individual of one sex with two or more individuals of the other sex more permanent than the irregular attachments that the solitary females form in order to lay fertile eggs.

A male Red-crowned Ant-Tanager in Belize had two mates and two nests at the same time. The only other case of un-doubted bigamy that I know of among tanagers occurred at a nest of Blue-grays with four eggs—twice the almost invariable number in southern Costa Rica, where this nest was found. The two females who attended the eggs kept them continuously covered. The dominant female, A, sat when she wanted to, with the constancy of a Blue-gray Tanager incubating alone; the subordinate female, B, sat only when the other permitted her to occupy the nest. Tanager B always meekly jumped from the nest as A, returning from a recess, approached it; once, when B was slow to leave, she received a peck on the head, which explained why she looked so unkempt. While A incubated, B spent much time hopping around the nest or preening nearby, obviously desiring to sit on the eggs but unable to do so. B rested once, for a minute, on the nest's rim with her breast over A. The moment A stretched her wings and left the nest for an outing, B would sit in it, with the result that the eggs were left uncovered for only an instant.

The bigamous male Blue-gray Tanager fed A on the nest three or four times a morning, but he gave nothing to B while she sat. This bestowal of gifts did not necessarily indicate his partiality to A. He usually accompanied whichever female was out foraging. Whenever he returned with A, B would vacate the nest before she could be fed there; but when he returned with B, A would continue to occupy the nest and receive whatever food he had brought. Female B, who perforce incubated less than one-third of the time that A did, was with the male much more and

Blue-gray Tanager *Thraupis episcopus*
Sexes alike. Central Mexico to Bolivia and Amazonian Brazil.

may have been fed by him when they were beyond view. It was interesting to find the dominant individual insisting on taking the major share of the task of incubation, leaving the other free to roam with the male. All four of the eggs hatched, but only two of the young survived until they were feathered, and they left the nest at an earlier age than do most Blue-gray Tanagers.

Table 2. Clutch size, incubation periods, and nestling periods of tanagers

Species	Clutch size[1]	Incubation period (days)[1]	Nestling period (days)[1]	Locality
Silver-throated Tanager	2	13.25	15 (14–16)	Costa Rica
Speckled Tanager	2	ca. 13	15	Costa Rica
Bay-headed Tanager	2	13–14	15–16	Costa Rica
Golden-masked Tanager	2	13–16	14–16	Costa Rica, Panama
Blue Dacnis	2	—	12	Costa Rica
Green Honeycreeper	2	12.5–13	12	Costa Rica
Shining Honeycreeper	2	12–13	13–14	Costa Rica
Red-legged Honeycreeper	2	12–13	14	Costa Rica
Golden-browed Chlorophonia	3	—	23–25	Costa Rica
Yellow-throated Euphonia	5	16	17+	Guatemala
Yellow-crowned Euphonia	2–4	—	22–24	Costa Rica
Tawny-bellied Euphonia	2–3	17–18	20	Costa Rica
White-vented Euphonia	3 (4)	15–17	18–20	Costa Rica
Blue-gray Tanager	2 (1–3)	13–14 (12)	16–20	Costa Rica, Suriname
Palm Tanager	2 (3)	14	17–20	Trinidad
Gray-headed Tanager	2 (3)	14 (16)	11–12 (10)	Costa Rica
White-lined Tanager	(1) 2	14–15	—	Trinidad
Red-crowned Ant-Tanager	3 (2)	13–14	10	Belize
Red-throated Ant-Tanager	3 (2–4)	12–13.5	—	Belize
Crimson-backed Tanager	2	12	11	Panama
Scarlet-rumped Tanager	2 (3)	12.25 (13)	12 (11–14)	Costa Rica
Silver-beaked Tanager	2	12	11–12	Northern South America
Common Bush-Tanager	2	14	12–13	Costa Rica
Western Tanager	3–5	13	—	United States
Scarlet Tanager	4 (3–5)	13–14	15	United States
Summer Tanager	3–4 (5)	12?	—	United States

1. Less frequent numbers of eggs and less usual incubation and nestling periods (see chapter 9) are given in parentheses.

Probably the nest, built for two, was too small to accommodate four nestlings. I regretted that I had not discovered this nest before the eggs were laid, to learn whether continuous incubation would accelerate embryonic development.

The first indication that a tanager's eggs are about to hatch is a slight roughness of the shell at a point on or near the greatest transverse diameter. When the egg is held to the ear, slight tapping or crunching sounds may be audible. From about twelve to twenty-six hours after these first signs of pipping, the hatchling has severed the cap of the shell, pushes it off, and emerges.

Affected by an array of factors, the incubation periods of tanagers vary widely (Table 2). Short periods are found in *Ramphocelus*, whose nests are thick and well insulated but usually low in thickets, where they are exposed to heavy predation. In this genus, Scarlet-rumped Tanagers, for which we have the greatest number of careful determinations of the incubation period, hatch their eggs in 12 to 13 days, with an average of 12.25 days, counting from the laying of the second egg to the hatching of this egg. The related Crimson-backed and Silver-beaked tanagers have similar nests, and incubation periods approximately 12 days. In the slight, usually high nests of Red-legged, Shining, and Green honeycreepers, the incubation period is between 12 and 13 days. In the low, very thin nests of Gray-headed Tanagers, the eggs—about the size of those of the Scarlet-rumped Tanager— take 14 days to hatch. Possibly they need two days longer because they are poorly insulated, possibly also because they are left exposed for relatively long intervals while the female parent goes off to find and forage with army ants. In the thick, usually rather high, and well-hidden nests of Silver-throated, Speckled, Bay-headed, and Golden-masked tanagers and other species of *Tangara*, as in the well-padded and often high nests of Blue-gray Tanagers, the incubation period is 13 to 14 days. In cool highland forests, the eggs of Common Bush-Tanagers hatch in 14 days. By far the longest incubation periods recorded in the family are those of the euphonias, whose tiny eggs in covered, usually well-concealed, often high nests sometimes hatch in 15 or 16 days but often take 17 to 18 days.

Soon after the hatchling tanagers emerge from the eggs, their mother eats the empty shells or carries them away in her bill.

9 Nestlings and Their Care

A hatchling tanager squirms out of its shell with its down, moist with egg fluids, plastered against its skin in thick, curly strands. The down soon dries in the heat of the brooding mother and spreads apart in loose clusters of gray filaments, gossamer fine and too sparse to conceal the nestling's pink skin. The euphonia's natal down is so scanty and short that it hardly shades the tiny birdling's shiny black skin.

Lying in the bottom of the nest with its head bent under, a newly hatched tanager appears too weak and frail to be capable of movement; but soon it trembles, struggles as though trying to lift a crushing weight, straightens its neck, lifts its sightless head in the air, and, quivering with the effort, opens wide its mouth, revealing a bright red or orange-red interior. Projecting folds of skin at the corners of the mouth, white in many tanagers, yellow in bush-tanagers, contrast with the vivid interior and may make it more attractive to parents bringing food. On the ridge of the upper mandible, near the tip, is an egg tooth so minute that it easily escapes notice. This tiny projection has helped the chick break out of the shell. Instead of falling away intact, like the larger egg teeth of gallinaceous and other birds, it gradually disappears while the nestling tanager is growing.

Heeding the voiceless plea for nourishment, the mother does not delay long to feed her nestling; sometimes, if it hatches during the night or at dawn, she brings food while the light seems too dim for finding it. Patiently she offers very small items to a nestling whose slowness in swallowing food often contrasts with its apparent eagerness for it. As far as is known, males of all species of tanagers, including euphonias and honeycreepers, help their mates to nourish the nestlings. How does the male parent, who does not incubate and has been less closely associated with the nest than his partner, learn that nestlings who need food have hatched? Careful watching at nests of tanagers and a number of other passerine birds has failed to reveal any indication that the female deliberately informs her mate of this important event, as by a special call or gesture. The male must discover by other means that he has become a father with work to do.

The male parent's promptness in making the discovery depends greatly on the habits he has formed while his partner incubated. If he has been feeding her at the nest, bringing food and presenting it to the eggs in anticipation of their hatching, making visits of inspection, or accompanying his mate as she returns to her eggs after an outing, he may find the nestlings with little delay. If his visits to the nest during incubation have been widely spaced but, nevertheless, he promptly begins to feed the nestlings, he has probably been alerted by clues that do not depend on such visits, such as seeing the nestlings' mother collect food in her bill or deliver it at the nest or observing her increased eagerness to receive food from him.

In the gray dawn of a misty May morning, a female Golden-masked Tanager whose eggs had been pipped early in the preceding afternoon sat restlessly, repeatedly rising up to look down into her mossy nest in the fork of a calabash tree. Before sunrise, she ate the big part and then the cap of an empty shell, a clear indication that at least one of her eggs had hatched. Thrice she flew off for a brief outing, to return without anything for her nestlings. While brooding, she exchanged calls with her mate, apparently without informing him of the birth of his offspring. After another short absence she returned with food, closely attended by her partner. As she perched near the nest, he hovered momentarily above it and had his first view of the hatchlings. While she fed them, he hunted over a neighboring mossy branch, found a spider, and for two minutes tried to induce a nestling to swallow it. Not succeeding, apparently because it was too big for the tiny hatchling, he passed the spider to the mother, who ate it. Thus, each of the parents brought food for the young at nearly the same time, fifty and fifty-one minutes after the female had eaten the shell. Although the female's calls did not incite the male to bring food, the sight of the nestlings stimulated him to do so without delay.

Nearly two years later, a pair of Golden-masked Tanagers again nested in the same mossy fork of the calabash tree. Again the nestlings hatched before sunrise, and again the female first fed them on her fourth return from brief outings, an hour after she had eaten the empty shells. In the second hour of the morning she fed the nestlings five times, while her mate, who often accompanied her to near the nest and exchanged calls with her, brought nothing. More than two hours after the eggs had hatched, he perched above the nest while she gave the young their sixth meal, saw them for the first time, and promptly found an insect for them. As at the earlier nest, the father fed his brood a few minutes after he first saw them and thereafter was a regular provider.

Once, in the early dawn, while the light was still so dim that my eyes could hardly follow her movements, a female Silver-throated Tanager carried, one by one, four pieces of empty shell from her mossy nest and appeared to feed her two hatchlings. Despite vocal contact with his mate, the male delayed long to feed his offspring. Finally, nearly two and a half hours after the mother had delivered the first meal, the pair returned together, each bringing food. The male preceded his mate to the nest and, clinging to a thick, mossy branch above it and stretching far downward, fed the nestlings for the first time. Since he had been in the habit of feeding his incubating partner at rather long intervals, I did not take his arrival with food as evidence that he was already aware of his progeny. Nevertheless, the fact that on arriving with an insect in his bill he preceded his partner to the nest suggests that he had foreknowledge of the nestlings. Probably he learned that a change had occurred by finding food in his partner's bill when he offered to feed her among the trees.

The female Scarlet-rumped Tanager usually eats the empty eggshells instead of carrying them away in her bill. At one nest, the father first brought food only thirty-eight minutes after the first egg had hatched. At another nest the interval was ninety-two minutes. Other males, less attentive, have taken much longer to find their nestlings; one did not bring food until nearly five hours after the hatching. Two others delayed until the following day; but at one of these nests the first egg hatched on a rainy afternoon instead of in the morning, which is more usual.

At four of five nests, the father came with food before he saw the nestlings. Male Scarlet-rumped Tanagers have not been seen to feed their mates; but sometimes, as has been said, they offer food to unhatched eggs. The males' arrival with food for young they have not seen may be no more than anticipatory food-bringing, but this occurs at such long intervals that I believe another explanation must be sought for early feeding of newly hatched nestlings. Probably the father is prompted to bring food to the nest by seeing the mother carry it. Perhaps only males with previous experience in breeding learn in this manner that nestlings have hatched and promptly feed them. As they grow older and gain experience in breeding, birds of many kinds become more efficient parents, and more of their young survive.

In the first spurt of feeding, male parents may bring more food than tiny nestlings can eat. The excess may then go to their mother, who thereby is enabled to brood more continuously, which in inclement weather may save the young from debilitating or lethal exposure. Often the father spends much time coaxing hatchlings to swallow items too big for them or to accept food when they are satiated. Male Scarlet-rumped Tanagers sometimes continue for as much as five or six minutes to present a morsel to nestlings, the while repeating low, sharp, or squeaky notes or a subdued version of their song. After a while male parents learn to adjust their offerings to the young birds' capacity. From the first, females tend to select more appropriate items. The first meals they bring to the nest are often small enough to be carried inside the mouth or throat, although with the exception of euphonias and chlorophonias, tanagers are not known to regurgitate to their nestlings. If the young have difficulty swallowing an item, the parent mashes it in its bill before presenting it again or transfers it from one mouth to another until it disappears.

On the day her nestlings hatched, a female Silver-throated Tanager swallowed fragments of her nest's lining—extraordinary behavior that has been reported also of the Northern Gannet. In addition to eating a piece of dry, papery leaf from the bottom of her nest, the Silver-throat billed or tried to swallow other fragments, which she eventually dropped back into the cup or carried away. Four times she flew away with pieces of leaf, probably because some of the leaves had curled up around the nestlings and interfered with her attendance on them. A White-vented Euphonia also swallowed fragments of her nest's lining.

Some male birds have trouble finding the nest. On the morning that a Tawny-bellied Euphonia's eggs hatched, the male returned with his mate and preceded her to the dangling mass of bromeliads and other epiphytes into which the nest was tucked. For nearly a quarter of an hour he searched for the doorway, clinging here and there to the pendent mass, sometimes peering down from a point so near the entrance that he seemed almost able to look into it. At intervals he flew to neighboring branches, then returned to renew the search. He hovered beside the nest but not in the proper position to see inside. After hunting fruitlessly in the mass that contained the nest, he examined small epiphytes and debris on surrounding dangling roots. Finally, he gave up and left. Later in the morning and again on the following day he resumed his search, with no better success. I could not learn whether he would finally have succeeded, for on the afternoon of this second day the nestlings vanished, probably swallowed by a snake or other predator with keener senses than the nestlings' father, who obviously wished to feed them but could not find them. If he was the same bird who had helped build this nest three months earlier, had often escorted his partner to the doorway while she was incubating, and had fed the first brood in it, his memory was short. After this earlier brood had hatched, the male, whether the same or a different individual, did not feed the nestlings until they were about three days old. Birds, like people, differ in alertness and efficiency.

Whole berries and bits of larger fruits, arillate seeds, and insects nourish nestling tanagers. Parents often bring several items at one time, the smaller ones inside the mouth or throat, the larger ones projecting from the bill. Insects are usually so badly mangled that to identify them is difficult, but green grasshoppers, caught in the grass, are often recognizable in the thick bluish bills of parent Scarlet-rumped Tanagers. Honeycreepers frequently come to their nests with red or orange arils lined up conspicuously the whole length of their long, slender black bills, or with small blue or black berries similarly arranged, the outer-

Table 3. Rates of parental feeding of nestling tanagers

Species	Number of nestlings	Age (days)	Hours watched	Number of feedings			Meals per nestling per hour
				Male	Female	Total	
Silver-throated Tanager	2	4	6	25	32	57	4.8
Silver-throated Tanager	2	11	6	34	48	82	6.8
Speckled Tanager	1	3	6.5	17	13	30	4.6
Speckled Tanager	2	11–12	9.75	—	—	118[1]	6.0
Golden-masked Tanager	2	4–14	5	36	29	65	6.5
Green Honeycreeper	2	4	6	7	26	33	2.8
Green Honeycreeper	2	9	6	14	36	50	4.2
Shining Honeycreeper	2	1–2	6	17	22	39	3.2
Shining Honeycreeper	2	7–8	6	31+	36+	70[1]	5.8
Red-legged Honeycreeper	2	2–11	11.75	35	97	132	5.6
Tawny-bellied Euphonia	2	2	6	0	9	9	0.75
Tawny-bellied Euphonia	2	9–16	12	16	16	32	1.33
White-vented Euphonia	3	4–5	6	10	11	21	1.17
White-vented Euphonia	3	12–16	16	32	32	64	1.33
Gray-headed Tanager	2	10	4	—	—	32[1]	4.0
Red-crowned Ant-Tanager	2	8	5	12	17	30[1]	3.0
Scarlet-rumped Tanager	2	4–7	23	95	203	298	6.5
Scarlet-rumped Tanager	2	7–13	29.5	107	254	361	6.1
Scarlet-rumped Tanager	3	5–11	22	137	266	403	6.1
Scarlet-rumped Tanager	1	7–12	8	0	64	64	8.0
Crimson-backed Tanager	2	3–10	10	26	27	53	2.7
Silver-beaked Tanager	1	6	4	0	21	21	5.3
Common Bush-Tanager	2	5	4.25	—	—	29[1]	3.5

1. Both parents fed the nestlings, but either they were indistinguishable or the light was poor.

most projecting from the tip of the bill and making it appear longer than it is.

Although, with the exception of occasional nests of Scarlet-rumped and Silver-beaked tanagers belonging to females without mates, males of all members of the family which have been studied attend the young, usually they bring fewer meals than females do (Table 3). Female Scarlet-rumped Tanagers and Red-legged Honeycreepers commonly feed their young from two to three times as often as do their colorful partners. In Michigan, male Scarlet Tanagers accounted for only 37 percent of 758 feedings at several nests. In Belize, male Red-crowned Ant-Tanagers brought 14.7 percent of 469 meals; male Red-throated Ant-Tanagers, 33 percent of 397 meals. When a male arriving with food finds his mate brooding the nestlings, he may pass his billful to her for delivery to them, or she may rise up or leave so he can reach them. If she persists in sitting tight, he may wait patiently beside the nest until she departs. A male Shining Honeycreeper waited nearly a quarter of an hour for the opportunity to feed two-day-old nestlings.

The number of meals brought to a tanager's nest in a single hour fluctuates widely. Longer periods of recording reveal more uniformity in rates of feeding. Four to six meals per hour for each of the nestlings, at least after they are about two days old, is usual for many tanagers and honeycreepers. Scarlet-rumped Tanagers feed their young about as often during the first as during the second half of their lives in the nest—slightly over six times per nestling per hour—compensating for the greater need of older nestlings by bringing larger rather than more frequent meals. Tanagers that seldom lay more than two eggs are capable of raising three young. At rare nests of Scarlet-rumped Tanagers with three nestlings—sometimes the offspring of two females— the rate of feeding per nestling was only slightly less than with broods of two. Trios of nestlings fed by two parents left the nest at the usual age and appeared in every way normal.

In an experiment, nestlings of about the same age in neighboring nests were temporarily shifted back and forth, so that on consecutive mornings one of the nests held two, then three, then one. The parents adjusted their rates of feeding so well that for the two, three, and one young the average hourly rates were, respectively, 7.5, 7.1, and 7.2 meals for each nestling. As has been demonstrated at nests of birds of other families, the rate of food delivery is determined primarily by demand, as revealed especially by the clamor the nestlings make at mealtime. At the experimental nest the noise of three nestlings stimulated the male, a poor provider, to feed them more than twice as often as when only one or two were present. Solitary females with a single nestling fed it at the rate of eight times an hour, substantially more often than the rate at nests with two nestlings and two attendants. Single nestlings need more food for heat production than do those in larger broods; the latter, by huddling together, help keep one another warm.

Unlike other tanagers, euphonias and chlorophonias regularly approach their nests with nothing visible in their bills and feed

Hooded Tanager *Nemosia pileata*
Male. Tropical South America.

their young by regurgitation—as they do their mates. When a
parent alights in the doorway of one of the covered nests, two,
three, or more mouths open in front of it like red flowers on
waving stalks. Promptly the adult proceeds to regurgitate food
and deposit it in these corollas, a little at a time, first in one and
then in another. The short parental bill is not inserted deeply
into a nestling's throat, as it is in hummingbirds. To regurgitate,
the parent retracts its neck and jerks its head up and down or
twitches it sideward. Looking sharply through a good binocular,
one can discern a bulge traveling up the foreneck. On a single
visit, each parent delivers this soft pabulum in about four to
thirty (but mostly eight to twelve) portions, or separate acts of
regurgitation.

Birds that feed their young by regurgitation, such as certain
woodpeckers, do so much less frequently than do species in the
same family that feed directly from the bill. Euphonias conform

to this rule, delivering meals about one-fourth as often as other tanagers, apparently compensating for lower frequency by making them more copious and nourishing. The rate of feeding increases only slightly as nestling euphonias grow older; and, as in pigeons, the duration of meals is reduced, probably because food is regurgitated more rapidly to larger young that can swallow it faster. At the nest of a pair of White-vented Euphonias with three five-day-old young, a parent took fifty to ninety-four seconds to deliver a meal; when the same young were fifteen days old, the time was reduced to between thirteen and thirty-five seconds. After a meal a large, dark swelling on the front and right side of each nestlings neck reveals where the food is stored awaiting digestion. The same kind of swelling appears in hummingbirds and others fed by regurgitation.

Because they keep such close company, male and female euphonias tend to feed their nestlings with equal frequency. Nearly always they come to the nest together, and the male goes first to cling in the doorway and regurgitate to the nestlings. After he returns to perch near his waiting partner, she feeds them. If she does not stay to brood, they fly away together. Rarely do the two parents feed the nestlings simultaneously in the narrow doorway. As long as brooding continues, this order of feeding avoids unnecessary motion; if the female fed first, she would have to leave the nest to permit her partner to feed, then return to brood. However, the same order persists throughout the nestling period, long after brooding ceases, when no reason for it is apparent. And as for unnecessary motion, frequently the male, after feeding the nestlings and returning to his perch, closely escorts his partner as she flies to the nest, just as he had done each time she entered to incubate the eggs. She may also fly beside him to the doorway, so strong is the euphonias' habit of accompanying their consorts.

This sequence of feeding the nestlings pervails not only among euphonias and chlorophonias, with their closed nests, but also among certain tanagers with open nests. When a pair of Golden-masked Tanagers or Silver-throated Tanagers arrive with food at about the same time, the male nearly always delivers his contribution first, even after brooding has ceased. Scarlet-rumped parents usually come separately with food, so no order of feeding develops. The males and females of many species of tanagers are so similar that it is difficult to learn who goes first.

After being fed, a nestling often turns around to deliver a dropping to the parent. The feces of most tanagers are voided in a gelatinous sac, which facilitates removal. The parent may either swallow it, as happens most frequently with younger nestlings, or carry it away in the bill to drop at a distance. Euphonias enjoy no such convenience. After feeding, a parent of either sex waits in the doorway until one or more nestlings turn to present their rear ends, from which oozes a gelatinous or watery stuff containing small seeds and fragments of tiny insects, which the parent eats little by little, appearing almost to lick it up with its tongue. Sometimes the male euphonia, after waiting nearby while his mate feeds, pushes into the doorway beside her and assists in removing the excrement. It is never carried away visibly in their bills. Sometimes the fecal matter pulls out in long, clear strings, like that of adult euphonias. This colorless viscid matter appears to be from mistletoe seeds, which figure largely in the euphonias' diet. It sticks the seeds to tree branches, where they germinate and push suckers through bark and wood to draw sap from the host plant.

Incubating the eggs and brooding the nestlings are similar occupations; birds who do not incubate rarely brood. If the male parent begins promptly to feed the newly hatched nestlings, their mother may brood them almost as constantly as she covered the eggs. Now, however, both her sessions and her absences, during which she seeks food for herself and her young, tend to be shorter and less regular. If she receives no help in provisioning her brood, her time in the nest may be reduced. As the days pass, the mother broods less and less until, when the nestlings are seven or eight days old and have some ability to regulate their own temperature, she warms them little on fair days. A hard shower, however, may send her to cover them even after they are well feathered and so completely fill the bowl that she rests above rather than in it.

Many birds that breed in covered nests, holes, or burrows cease to brood their nestlings by night before they are feathered. This practice reduces the risk that both parents and young will be trapped by a predator that blocks the exit. When euphonias are only eight or nine days old, they sleep without the maternal coverlet. Although their roofed nest gives some protection from the nocturnal rains frequent during their breeding season, they seem too tiny and naked to be left alone. Nevertheless, even at this early age they feel warm after nightfall. Hummingbirds at about the same age are left uncovered at night, in open cups rather than nests with roofs, and they suffer no harm even at moderate altitudes where nocturnal rains are chilly.

Tanagers with open nests continue nighttime brooding longer. Scarlet-rumped, Crimson-backed, Silver-beaked, and Gray-headed tanagers and Green Honeycreepers cover their nestlings through the night until they are eleven or twelve days old and ready to depart; at most (unless disturbed) they may leave the nestlings alone on their last night in the nest. Golden-masked and Silver-throated tanagers continue nocturnal brooding about as long as these larger tanagers do; but since the nestling period is longer, the young often sleep alone during their final three or four nights in the nest.

As we have seen, tanagers hatch with closed eyes and (except euphonias) pink skin hardly concealed by fairly long, sparse, gray natal down. To follow their development, let us take the Scarlet-rumped Tanager, whose often low nests, close to human dwellings, favor observation. At the age of three days, the nestlings' eyelids begin to separate, and the horny sheaths that enclose the remiges begin pushing out from the rear edges of the wings. When lifted from the nest, the nestlings may utter a weak peep—their first sound. By their fifth day they can open their eyes wide; the pins of their longer wing feathers (remiges and their greater coverts) have become conspicuously long; and pinfeathers are sprouting on their bodies. When they are six days old, all their feathers are still enclosed. A day later the remiges and some body feathers are escaping from the ends of their sheaths; the less advanced head and tail feathers are still enclosed. On eight-day-old nestlings the body feathers are quite generally shedding their sheaths. At nine days the nestlings are rapidly becoming feathered. By the twelfth day after hatching, Scarlet-rumped Tanagers, well plumaged, with wing feathers

sufficiently expanded for weak flight but with tails still rudi-
mentary, are ready to leave the nest.

Nestling Silver-throated, Golden-masked, and Gray-headed
tanagers, Common Bush-Tanagers, Red-legged and Green honeycreepers, and several other members of the family develop at
about the same rate as Scarlet-rumped Tanagers. The development of euphonias is much slower. Their eyes do not begin to
open until they are eight or nine days old. At ten days they are
fully open. By the nestlings' ninth day the pins of their wing
plumes have become long, but the body feathers are just emerg-
ing from the skin. At twelve days of age, when larger tanagers
leave the nest well clothed, euphonias are still nearly naked. A
day later their plumage begins to shed its horny sheaths, and at
fifteen days they are fairly well covered except on the head.

Fledgling tanagers leave their nests spontaneously, without
parental urging, most often in the forenoon. Most Scarlet-
rumped Tanagers depart when twelve days old, fewer at thirteen
days, very few at eleven days. The nests of some that stayed
fourteen or fifteen days were so situated that horses and cows
had often disturbed their incubating or brooding parent by day
and night. These Scarlet-rumps were at an altitude of about
twenty-five hundred feet (750 m) above sea level, where nights
are cool. At lower and warmer altitudes, Scarlet-rumped, Silver-
beaked, and Crimson-backed tanagers severed contact with their
nests when eleven days old.

Golden-masked Tanagers and other callistes, whose nests tend
to be higher and less conspicuous, do not leave the nest until
fourteen to sixteen days of age, usually about fifteen. Unless disturbed, Blue-gray Tanagers cling to their often high and well-hidden nests until they are sixteen to twenty days old. Euphonias,
in keeping with their slow development, linger in their snug
nests for the first eighteen to twenty-four days of their lives;
chlorophonias have an equally long nestling period. Among altricial birds, the longer the incubation period, the longer the young
tend to remain in the nest.

After leaving the nest, whether capable of flying weakly or
fairly well, young tanagers disappear: low-nesting species, such
as the Scarlet-rumped, conceal themselves in dense thickets;

those that nest and fly higher take shelter in the foliage of trees. The parents diligently carry food to these fledglings, however difficult to find. After hiding for two or three weeks, the juveniles, already flying well, follow their parents about, often to the feeder, where with fluttering wings they take the food that complaisant elders place in gaping mouths. We have little information on how long young tanagers continue to be fed. A six-week-old Crimson-backed Tanager clumsily dropped the berries it plucked and tried to eat, then quivered its wings and called for food, reminding me of a little child who, after failing to accomplish a task beyond its strength and skill, petulantly cries for adult assistance. The young bird's father still carried food to it, while its mother incubated her second brood. A Speckled Tanager was still being fed at the age of forty-five days. Red-throated Ant-Tanagers in Belize apparently became independent at about thirty days; although after reaching this age they sometimes begged from a parent, they were not seen to be fed.

When the young tanagers emerge from hiding and follow their parents, they are almost full grown and resemble their mother if she is much duller than their father. If both parents are highly colored, as in many callistes, the juveniles tend to be plainer, with greenish, yellowish, or olive plumage. When both parents are equally plain, the juveniles do not differ greatly from them. Soon after becoming self-supporting, but sometimes while still closely associated with their parents, young Scarlet-rumped Tanagers, Golden-masked Tanagers, Red-legged Honeycreepers, and others begin to acquire adult colors by completely changing their body plumage. Before the following breeding season, at least in southern Costa Rica, all males of these species, yearlings as well as older birds, are in full nuptial attire. I have never seen a male with traces of immaturity attending a nest, although once a most exceptional female Golden-masked Tanager bred in a plumage that was not fully adult.

In keeping with their generally slower development, male euphonias and chlorophonias take longer to acquire adult colors and often breed in plumage intermediate between that of females and older males, as do Bicolored Conebills in Trinidad. Little is known about the plumage changes of most tropical tanagers. Fledglings of the three migratory northern tanagers—the Scarlet, Summer, and Western—differ from their mothers not only in being duller but in having dark streaks or spots on their whitish or yellowish underparts. Young males fly southward in plumage not greatly different from that of females and acquire bright adult colors in their winter homes, but they may return to the north and nest while still bearing traces of immaturity.

Tanagers have been most intensively studied in the northern tropics, above nine degrees of latitude. There they breed mainly in the first months of the rainy season, from March or April to July or August, with a scattering of nests before or after this period. In Trinidad, at about ten degrees north latitude, Blue-gray, Palm, and Silver-beaked tanagers breed through most or all of the year but with by far the greatest number of nests from March to August. In Suriname, nearer the equator, nests of Blue-gray and Silver-beaked tanagers have been found in every month.

The breeding seasons of many tropical tanagers are long enough to rear several broods; but more nests fail than succeed in fledging young, and many nests are built after a failure. True second broods, following a successful nest, are probably frequent among tanagers. They have been recorded of Scarlet-rumped, Crimson-backed, Golden-masked, Silver-throated, Gray-headed, Palm, and Blue-gray tanagers; White-vented and Tawny-bellied euphonias; and Golden-browed Chlorophonias. In predator-ridden tropical forests and thickets, a pair of tanagers who rear more than two broods in a season, no matter how often they try, must be exceptionally shrewd at concealing their nests or exceptionally lucky. Among the shrewd or lucky ones was a pair of Palm Tanagers in Trinidad; in nests well hidden in a palm tree the two raised four broods and lost one in less than a year. In later years, half of their four nests failed. One year, a pair of Blue-gray Tanagers in our garden laid four sets of eggs between March and July without rearing a single fledgling. Tanagers frequently lay again in a nest from which they have lost eggs or nestlings.

10 Helpers

Birds that feed or in any other way aid other birds that are neither their mates nor their dependent young are known as helpers, or sometimes auxiliaries. Helpers are rarely nestlings, frequently juveniles, often yearlings or older nonbreeding adults, and occasionally parents with eggs or young of their own. When the beneficiaries belong to their own species, their benefactors are designated intraspecific helpers; when birds serve individuals or broods of a different species, they are named interspecific helpers; when several birds share a nest, incubate by turns the double or larger clutch, and feed the nestlings indiscriminately, they are called mutual helpers. Intraspecific helpers are most frequent among the continuously resident birds of the tropics and subtropics. However, a constantly increasing number in the most diverse families is found nearly everywhere that birds are intensively studied, not excluding the Arctic tundra. Interspecific helpers are most often reported in temperate North America and Europe where most bird-watchers live. Tanagers produce their share of helpers, both intraspecific and interspecific, although no breeding system as complex as that of certain jays, babblers, starlings, and others has yet been found among them—perhaps because the great majority of species remain to be studied.

Throughout the year, lovely Golden-masked Tanagers wander in closely associated pairs, or sometimes in groups of three or four birds in adult plumage, through the upper levels of rain forests and into clearings with scattered trees, shady plantations, and gardens. When pairs nest, the male helps his mate in all domestic tasks, with the exception of incubation. So many Golden-masks' nests are lost that these tanagers seem seldom to rear two broods in a year. When they do hatch a second brood, a juve-

86

nile of the earlier brood may help the parents to attend the later one. At one nest in Panama and three in Costa Rica, I watched Golden-masks in greenish juvenile plumage, plain or flecked with the brighter colors of adults, bring food to nestlings. One of these young helpers began bringing food when it was only forty-six days old. It also carried away fecal sacs. Often the juvenile arrived at the nest with its two parents, but occasionally it came alone. It brought smaller items than the parents did, and its attendance was irregular, with intervals of feeding (about as frequently as an adult) alternating with periods of neglect, as though it found grown-up activity tiring. Apparently, it did not consistently find enough food for itself, for with fluttering wings it begged from its parents, without, as far as I saw, receiving anything. Sometimes juvenile Golden-masks try to help their parents build a later nest, as by gathering materials that they drop or making shaping movements in the bowl, all without contributing anything substantial to the undertaking.

In three localities I watched trios of Golden-masked Tanagers in fully adult plumage attend nestlings. One trio brought food to a nest with one nestling and one unhatched egg, which made it appear improbable that two females had laid in this nest. One September, through my study window, I frequently saw four adults carrying food to a late nest. They arrived in pairs more often than all together, but when four were at the nest, I noticed no antagonism. I could not learn the number of young in this high nest, set deeply amid the long, sharp-tipped leaves of an arborescent *Yucca;* nor could I tell the relationship of the nest's attendants.

Slowly, with her mate's help, one female Speckled Tanager, whose right leg hung useless, built a nest that was unusually frail and shallow. One of the two eggs that she laid fell from the slight structure, but despite her severe impediment, she hatched the other in fifteen days. While feeding the nestling, she rested her right wing against the nest's rim to help support herself. Soon the parents were joined by a helper, whom I had not seen during the building and incubation. The voluntary assistant, an adult indistinguishable from the nestling's father, sometimes came to the nest with the parents but more often went its own way. During nine hours of the young tanager's final days in the nest, it was fed 114 times—about as frequently as a brood of two—62 times by its father and the helper and 52 times by its crippled mother, who was certainly doing her share. After the fledgling flew, at the age of fifteen days, three adults—the female with the injured leg, the father, and the helper—took banana to it from the feeder. Between breeding seasons, four or five Speckled Tanagers often fly together.

The Plain-colored Tanager, an unadorned gray member of an ornate genus, inhabits humid forests from Costa Rica to Colombia. In a narrow clearing amid the forests of Panama, I watched four grown birds, all alike in appearance and often arriving in a little flock, feed two nestlings. I could not learn how the helpers were related to the parents.

The blue, black, turquoise, and yellow Turquoise Tanager, widely spread over South America from Colombia and Venezuela to Bolivia and Brazil, lives in closely knit groups of four to seven, or sometimes more, and rarely forages alone. On the island of Trinidad, four or five adults attend nestlings and feed fledglings. Although the nesting of this tanager has not been carefully studied, it appears that a pair separate from their associates while they build the nest and incubate the eggs; but after the eggs hatch, the whole group cares for the young until they become independent.

From southern Mexico through much of Central America to northern Colombia, Red-throated Ant-Tanagers forage in noisy family groups at the edges of forests and in second-growth woods, mangrove swamps, and plantations. Occasionally a non-breeding bird brings materials and works on the nest that a female is building in a shrub or small tree of the woodland undergrowth. After the eggs hatch, the parents, other adult females, and juveniles feed the nestlings. One juvenile brought food about as frequently as either parent did, but such assistance appears to be rare. Likewise, a male Red-throated Ant-Tanager repeatedly fed his neighbor's two nestlings, despite their father's opposition.

One might expect that Scarlet-rumped Tanagers—who live in loose flocks, do not defend territories, and often build two or

Helpers   89

more nests close together—would frequently serve as helpers, but I have noticed only one slight instance of this behavior in many hours of watching. A full-grown juvenile, afflicted with paralysis, was fed at least once by each of two females, one of whom appeared to be its parent; the other was the mother of fledglings just out of the nest.

In baskets of ferns hanging around a house close beside a Panamanian forest, Thick-billed Euphonias dug niches in the soil to contain their nests. One nest with five young was frequently visited by three or four Thick-bills, who appeared to feed them. Traces of immaturity in the plumage of some of the male attendants suggested that they were yearling sons of the pair whose nest they visited. In the following year, with three occupied nests at the house and at least ten grown birds showing interest in them, the situation became too confusing for observers to learn how many visited any one nest. I have watched one or more nests of five species of euphonias without finding any indication of helpers, but the Thick-billed Euphonia appears to be different and would repay careful study.

At one of the two nests of the Blue Dacnis which I have seen, the male sometimes fed his mate while she incubated two speckled eggs. A second male, also in full nuptial attire, was sometimes nearby. After one of the eggs hatched, both males helped the female feed the nestling. During my nineteen hours of watching, spaced throughout the nestling period, the mother brought food fifty-one times and the two males together sixty-one times. Sometimes one of the latter chased the other, but often they were at the nest together with food. When I inspected the high nest with a mirror raised on a long pole, both males joined the mother in protesting my intrusion, all three complaining in low, weak notes. This could have been a case of polyandry, otherwise unknown in the tanager family, but more probably the male who was less closely associated with the female was an unmated helper.

In chapter 8, I told of a bigamous male Blue-gray Tanager whose two females alternately incubated a double set of eggs and fed four nestlings without discriminating among them. Since each of these females warmed eggs and nourished young not her own, the two became, by definition, mutual helpers; they are the only example I know of in the tanager family.

It is a pity that nests of Dusky-faced Tanagers are so hard to find in the tangled thickets where these big, plainly clad, yellow-eyed birds live, for from what I have seen of their social habits, I strongly suspect that they are more advanced cooperative breeders than any of the foregoing species with helpers, except possibly Turquoise Tanagers. Not daring to increase the risk of predation by cutting our way through dense, obstructing vegetation to the single known nest (described in chapter 7), my son and I watched it from the higher bank on the opposite side of the narrow woodland stream. Among the noisy flock of seven grown birds who frequented the vicinity, one would advance to the nest with a single insect in its sharp bill, deposit it in one of the two gaping red mouths that rose above the nest's rim, then vanish into the thicket so quickly that we rarely could keep more than two simultaneously in view as they brought food or flew back to concealment. In six morning hours, during which forty-three meals were delivered, and in later vigils, we failed to obtain convincing evidence that more than three of these indistinguishable tanagers were visiting the nest, but we strongly suspected that the number of attendants was greater. Beside a different stream, three Dusky-faced Tanagers carried food into a thicket, apparently for fledged young who lurked invisibly amid the low, lush vegetation.

One of the strongest of avian drives is to place food into begging avian mouths, for the survival of all altricial birds depends on this activity. So compelling is the appeal of a gaping nestling mouth that breeding birds occasionally neglect their own nests to feed a neighbor's young. Parent birds would more frequently have helpers if they did not repel the intrusion at their nests of other individuals, including sometimes their own independent young. Certainly many additional examples of nest helpers among nonaggressive, weakly territorial tanagers will be disclosed if more species can be studied before they are decimated or extinguished by the destruction of their habitats, by trapping, and by biocides.

In the midst of a long journey over high Costa Rican mountains, I delayed my companions for twenty minutes while I

Dusky-faced Tanager *Mitrospingus cassinii*
Sexes alike. Costa Rica to western Ecuador.

watched one of the two nests of Sooty-capped Bush-Tanagers
which I have found. It was embedded invisibly in a thick mass of
green moss growing on a slender, dangling branch of an epiphytic shrub in the mossy cloud forest. In this brief interval, I saw
three birds, all much alike in plumage, arrive together with food.
Two promptly entered the nest, emerged with empty bills, and
flew away. The third, apparently a juvenile, delayed near the
nest, holding food in its bill and fluttering its wings like a fledgling begging to be fed. It continued this activity until a single
adult arrived with food, whereupon it entered the opening in the
ball of moss, to emerge with nothing visible in its bill. Then the
bird who had just arrived fed the nestlings, and both flew away. I
concluded that at least three grown birds were attending this
nest of a species whose life history has not been studied.

During four days one April, a male Red-legged Honeycreeper

in full breeding plumage fed a fledgling Scarlet-rumped Tanager, about twice his size, on the feeder in front of our house. Again and again this strange pair returned to the board, where the honeycreeper stuffed his ward with pieces of banana and plantain, once six billfuls in rapid succession. He supplemented this fare with insects caught amid foliage. The honeycreeper insisted on pushing his long, sharp bill well down into the throat of the short-billed tanager, who seemed not to enjoy this method of receiving food. When satiated, the fledgling would turn its head away, whereupon the insistent helper would flit over its back from side to side, presenting morsels alternately on the right and on the left, until the fledgling flew away, its attendant following.

Often the tanager pursued the honeycreeper through neighboring trees, begging with open mouth and fluttering wings; but when the attendant started on a high flight, the fledgling, whose kind does not fly so high or far, did not follow. This young Scarlet-rumped Tanager was beginning to feed itself, and it also received at least occasional meals from an adult male who was apparently its father. It seemed, however, to prefer the gifts of the obliging honeycreeper. No female tanager was seen to feed the young bird. What separated helper and ward after the fourth day, we did not learn.

For at least two days in a later year, a female Red-legged Honeycreeper gave billfuls of banana from the feeder to a fledgling Yellow-green Vireo. But I know of only two other cases of a tanager feeding birds of a different species. Both of these interspecific helpers were male Scarlet Tanagers, and both sets of recipients were Chipping Sparrows. One fed nestling sparrows for several days, until his own young hatched. Years later, in a different locality, another took food to nestling sparrows whose parents tried to drive him away.

Sometimes nesting tanagers receive help from other species. Late one May, bustling activity in the spreading crown of a copalchí tree in a pasture drew my attention to the mossy green nest of Golden-masked Tanagers, hidden in the outer foliage, too high for me to reach. Continued watching revealed a pair of tanagers and a female Tropical Gnatcatcher flitting around the nest, which cradled two nestlings. Their red mouths showed clearly that they were tanagers, not gnatcatchers, whose nestlings' mouths are lined with yellow. The gnatcatcher attended the nestlings while her mate built a neat, lichen-encrusted cup ten feet (3 m) away in the same umbrageous tree. Contrary to the usual practice of gnatcatchers, she did not help him, having been diverted from this undertaking by the irresistible appeal of gaping nestling mouths.

While the parent tanagers most often arrived together, their bills laden with fruit pulp, the gnatcatcher diversified the nestlings' diet with tiny insects. She engaged in all parental activities: feeding, cleaning the nest, brooding the nestlings, and defending them—against their parents! If the parents arrived while she sat, not quite comfortably, on nestlings too big for her, she jumped from the nest and flitted around, darting at them in a defiant attitude, wings expanded and tail spread, displaying the white outer feathers. Sometimes she pursued the parents as they flew between the nest and the neighboring forest where they foraged. At first the parents mostly ignored their uninvited assistant; but as days passed and she became more possessive, aggressive, and annoying, while her attendance on the nestlings degenerated, they chased her mildly, without ever, as far as I saw, touching her. Until the young tanagers flew, twelve days after I had discovered this strange association, the gnatcatcher continued to feed them, while her mate, taking no interest in these nestlings, continued to work on the nest—in which, as far as I could learn, she never laid an egg.

11 Enemies, Nesting Success, and Longevity

In May some years ago, while I sat in the cabin where I write, agonized cries startled me. Looking out the door, I saw, in the colorful foliage of a croton shrub, a female Scarlet-rumped Tanager hanging by one wing from the jaws of a green snake and fluttering wildly. I doubted whether the yard-long serpent, hardly thicker than my middle finger, could swallow the bird. But sympathy overcame scientific curiosity; without waiting to observe the outcome of the encounter, I grabbed the first stick that came to hand and released the tanager. She flew off apparently uninjured and soon returned to her nest, where the tree snake had seized her while she was defending her egg. This was the only time I have seen a snake capture an adult bird, although I have watched tanagers, wrens, and wren-sized thornbirds peck snakes, including some much larger than this one, near their nests or at a distance from them, always avoiding the serpents' jaws.

Scarlet-rumped Tanagers have the greatest antipathy to snakes, the chief despoilers of their usually low nests. Their excited cries draw a crowd of other small birds to mob large serpents, including seven-foot (2-m) micas, and they more actively pursue smaller ones. Our garden, situated between a large tract of old forest and several acres of second-growth woods, is often invaded by snakes, most frequently in the season when nests are most abundant. The tanagers' protests and notes of alarm usually warn us of a serpent's presence in the daytime. One March evening the cries of a pair of Scarlet-rumps nesting beside the porch made me rush out in time to save newly laid eggs from a yard-long reddish brown snake on the point of swallowing them. After I removed the snake, the female tanager settled on her nest in the dusk. Early in the night she cried out, apparently in her

94

sleep, something she seldom did. I wondered whether birds dream, as horses and dogs appear to, and whether her recent experience had given her a nightmare.

While I sat at my microscope two days later, harsh scolding drew my attention to a pair of Scarlet-rumped Tanagers who were threatening a lance-headed tree snake at the foot of a shrub. The serpent fled to the neighboring privet hedge, with the tanagers pursuing it closely. After the snake climbed into the hedge, the female tanager approached so near that it struck out and appeared to hit her. Before I could arrive with a stick, the snake, which resembled a thin, brown vine, had vanished. I joined the birds in searching for it. With eyes sharper than mine, they found it and led me to it by scolding. When I struck at the snake with my machete, the wiry privet stems protected it. Again the serpent disappeared, and again the tanagers indicated its position farther along the hedge. Still shielded by the hedge, it eluded another blow and fled beyond our ken.

An hour later, another alarm among the tanagers! This time it was caused by a long, slender green snake in a calabash tree over which a vine had grown. The serpent vanished, but half an hour later the birds' renewed excitement disclosed its presence in another part of the vine. The creeper saved it from my blow. On the following day, the tanagers discovered still another kind of snake. No wonder so many of the nests in our garden were despoiled!

In June of the same year, Scarlet-rumped Tanagers again demonstrated their pertinacity in pursuing, and their boldness in attacking, the chief pillagers of their nests. The rasping notes of a female disclosed the presence of a four-foot (120-cm) green tree snake in the broad, leafy crown of the spreading mango tree beside my study, where her nest with two eggs was so well hidden that I had not previously noticed it. My efforts to knock the snake down with a long pole failed, but the tanager continued to harass it until it fell to the ground. Before I could catch the snake, it disappeared in the hedge. For the next few hours, the tanagers' complaints and scolds, renewed at intervals, distracted me from my writing. Going to investigate, I found them and other birds flitting excitedly around the snake high in the guava tree that supported the feeder. A female Scarlet-rumped Tanager twice nipped the snake's tail, while it retracted its head with widely open mouth, as though to strike. Again it escaped when I tried to reach it with a long pole. But the birds did not forget it; nor did they permit me to do so. Finally, they traced it to an orange tree, where I killed it to save their nests and restore tranquility to our dooryard.

Many years ago, a commotion in the foliage overhanging a stream where I bathed drew my attention to a female Scarlet-rumped Tanager crying loudly in a querulous, nasal voice while she flitted around a small green snake at her nest. If she did not actually touch the snake, she certainly came within an inch of it. Despite her frantic effort to drive it away, the serpent continued to swallow her eggs. One might suppose that birds who so bravely defend their nests would more often save them from at least the smaller snakes. But as I have repeatedly seen, a ravening snake, apparently insensitive to pain and danger, continues to swallow its prey even when mortally wounded. How can a small bird deter such a predator?

In Panama, a pair of Crimson-backed Tanagers, who from an earlier nest had lost two nestlings to two different snakes in less than twenty-four hours, repeated nasal complaints for several hours while a large black-and-yellow mica lay hidden in the grass near their replacement nest, containing two well-grown nestlings. The parents perched in a rosebush and, with heads turned to one side, peered with one eye into the grass below them. Guided by the tanagers, I found and killed the source of their distress. After its removal they looked again and again at the spot where their enemy had lurked for so long, to make sure that it was no longer present. They had become so agitated by the extended interval of tension and fear that they did not become calm in the next hour; they continued to call more than usual, completely neglecting their nestlings, who had crouched down motionless while in peril but now became active and called increasingly for food.

After snakes, the chief diurnal predators on birds' nests appear to be squirrels. In recent years cinnamon-bellied, or red-tailed, squirrels have become so numerous on our farm that they may well destroy as many nests as snakes do, but I have hesitated to control their numbers as perhaps I should. Garden Thrushes, also called Clay-colored Robins, dart at these pesky rodents until they scamper away; but I have not seen tanagers, who are considerably smaller than thrushes, do more than complain about them. Unlike many other birds, Scarlet-rumped and other tanagers do not try to lure flightless predators from their nests by distraction displays. The only tanager I have seen feign injury was a female Gray-headed Tanager with newly hatched nestlings. As I approached her low nest, she dropped to the ground and hopped haltingly away as though injured, but without beating her wings. Many another small bird has simulated helplessness far more convincingly.

Although toucans are mainly frugivorous, they devour eggs and nestlings when they find them, as tanagers are well aware. Scarlet-rumped Tanagers, who so valiantly attack snakes, avoid confrontations with the huge, brightly colored beaks of these much bigger birds. Even the largest and boldest of the flycatchers hesitate to touch these marauders while they plunder a nest, although they may buffet them while they fly and cannot turn their heads to defend their backs. Scarlet-rumped Tanagers precipitately abandon their nests when a Fiery-billed Aracari (a middle-sized toucan) comes into view. Even the voice of a distant aracari may cause them to depart discreetly, thereby avoiding the disclosure of their nests by leaving in sight of the enemy. Among the nocturnal predators on tanagers' nests are certainly snakes and probably also opossums and smaller marsupials, as well as weasels and other mammals, although none of these quadrupeds has been caught *in flagrante delicto*. Ants also destroy many nests, by day and by night.

While soaring gracefully high in the air, catching insects with their feet, Swallow-tailed Kites occasionally spy a bird's nest far below and swoop down to ravish it. One afternoon, while I sat on the porch with visitors, watching a pair of Golden-masked Tanagers attend two week-old nestlings in a calabash tree fifty feet (15 m) in front of us, a Swallow-tailed Kite suddenly dived down, seized the nest, and bore it upward along with its occupants. A Tropical Kingbird darted angrily at the kite the moment it took the nest but was unable to divert the plunderer. Rising high into the air, the raptor soared around on set wings, holding the nest in its talons while it extracted the nestlings with its beak. Then it dropped the nest, which drifted slowly earthward. Returning a few minutes later with food in their bills and finding only a mossy crotch where their nest had been, the parents searched for it over surrounding branches and forks. For the next hour, they returned again and again with food and sought nestlings to receive it. Sometimes birds continue for days to bring food to nests from which they have lost their young.

An occasional, unexpected enemy of Golden-masked and probably other small tanagers is the Blue-gray Tanager, which appropriates their nests for its own brood (as described in chapter 7).

Although domestic chickens are hardly enemies of nesting tanagers, some Scarlet-rumps treat them as such. At times two parents, voicing sharp, nasal cries, flutter close above the head of an approaching fowl. One female, whose nest was a yard (1 m) up in a shrub beside our porch, darted at any chicken who happened to be nearby as she approached or left the nest. Usually the fowls, including big roosters, squawked and ran away when threatened in this manner, but a hen with chicks refused to be intimidated. As though encouraged by her success, the female tanager formed the habit of menacing chickens on the other side of the lawn, yards from her nest. She was only bluffing; I never saw her strike one.

In the United States, tanagers have different enemies. The approach of a Blue Jay to the neighborhood of a nest of Scarlet Tanagers incites vigorous action by the parents, who strike these bigger birds with their wings, sometimes forcing them to the ground. Incautious behavior by a female tanager may betray her nest to a jay. When an incubating female flew directly from her nest to confront a Blue Jay who apparently had not previously noticed it, her action revealed the nest's location. In the absence of the male tanager to help defend it, the jay went straight to it and pecked into an egg.

American Crows, a more formidable threat, have two ways of finding Scarlet Tanagers' nests well hidden amid foliage. Ken-

Scarlet Tanager *Piranga olivacea* (above)
Male perched on a pin oak, *Quercus palustris*. Southern Canada and eastern
and central United States; in winter to northwestern Bolivia.
Blue Jay *Cyanocitta cristata* (below)
Southern Canada and eastern and central United States.

neth Prescott has called these methods "wait and watch" and "hunt and frighten." In contrast to their vigorous attacks on Blue Jays, male tanagers fall silent when they hear crows; females crouch down in their nests, facing the direction of the sound. A crow practicing the wait and watch method of nest detection arrives silently and perches inconspicuously in the tanagers' territory, watching until a parent reveals the location of its nest by flying to or from it, whereupon the black marauder goes directly to the nest to devour its contents or bear them away to its young. The hunt and frighten tactic is used by several crows advancing through the trees, cawing loudly, snapping half-open wings against their bodies, filling the woodland with a din terrifying even to a human observer. They look around for the effects of their racket until an incubating or brooding tanager, her attachment to her nest strained to the breaking point, dives over its side, thereby revealing it to the hunting crows, with expected results.

Although Scarlet Tanagers do not ordinarily protest the presence of chipmunks, when one of these small, squirrellike rodents approached a fledgling Brown-headed Cowbird who had fluttered down almost to the ground, its foster mother vigorously attacked this potential threat to her fosterling. She flew at the chipmunk and struck it with her wings, repeating this action whenever it ventured out from beneath the fallen tree that it frequented, until the little mammal retreated beneath the prostrate trunk and remained out of sight.

More subtle enemies of tanagers are parasitic cowbirds, who surreptitiously drop their eggs into nests of other birds. The victims of this practice incubate the intruded eggs and rear the alien young—unless, as is known to be the case with an increasing number of potential hosts, they are smart enough to throw out the cowbird's eggs or cover them over with nest materials, above which they lay their own eggs. Among the dupes of the Brown-headed Cowbird of North America are the three species of tanagers most widely distributed over the United States, the Scarlet, Summer, and Western, all of which have reared young cowbirds. The Bronzed Cowbird of the southwestern United States, Mexico, and Central America has seven known hosts among tanagers, including species of *Habia, Piranga,* and *Ram-phocelus.* Red-crowned Ant-Tanagers and Summer, Flame-colored, Red-headed, and Scarlet-rumped tanagers have raised the fosterlings.

As is to be expected, Shiny Cowbirds, widespread in South America, where most tanagers live, have parasitized the greatest number there. Of the seventeen species reported to be hosts of this cowbird, four—the Bicolored Conebill, Sayaca Tanager, Blue-and-yellow Tanager, and Silver-beaked Tanager—are known to have reared this cowbird's young. Cowbirds' eggs have apparently never been found in nests of any species of *Tangara,* by far the largest genus in the family. This absence of records may be due to the fact that nests of callistes have been studied chiefly in rain-forest regions, where cowbirds are rare or absent (except the Giant Cowbird, which specializes in larger hosts).

A Brown-headed Cowbird watches a potential host build her nest and follows the course of events in it. After the host begins to lay her eggs, the cowbird comes, usually at dawn, and very rapidly deposits one of her own eggs in the nest, often after removing one of the host's eggs. A stealthy approach and rapid laying are indispensable; if caught by the nest's owners, the parasite will be violently attacked. A male Scarlet Tanager joined a pair of Red-eyed Vireos in opposing a female cowbird at the vireos' nest, about forty-five feet (14 m) from his own. In an aggressive posture, he advanced and pecked the intruding cowbird while she sat in the vireos' nest.

Unlike nestlings of the European Cuckoo and some of its relatives, the nestling cowbird does not eject the host's eggs or nestlings from the nest but often grows up with the legitimate offspring. However, the young cowbird tends to be larger, demand more food, and grow more rapidly, to the detriment of the host's own nestlings. The removal of eggs by the adult cowbird and the fosterling's greater demand for food severely reduce the yield of the host's reproductive effort; as a rule, each cowbird fledgling is raised at the cost of one or more of the foster parents' own young. In Prescott's study of Scarlet Tanagers in Michigan, thirty-three tanagers' eggs and fifteen cowbirds' eggs were laid in seventeen nests. Thirteen tanagers' eggs and eight cowbirds' eggs hatched. Although the tanagers laid and hatched about twice as many of their own eggs, they raised to the age of fledging equal numbers of the two kinds of young—eight of each.

With so many animals hungry for tanagers' eggs and young, with cowbirds replacing the eggs with their own, and with miscellaneous disasters such as tilted or fallen nests, eggs knocked out by falling branches, and abandonment in consequence of sundry disturbances, tanagers do not often succeed in raising young in more than half of their nests or from as many as half of the eggs they lay. Table 4 gives the nesting success of five species in Costa Rica and one in Michigan. Since nests found at all stages include some with nestlings already hatched or almost ready to fledge, and these nests have escaped perils to which others have succumbed, this sample usually contains a higher proportion of successful nests than the smaller sample composed only of nests found early—before or at the beginning of incubation—and, accordingly, exposed to all perils for the whole period of occupancy. For this reason I have treated the two samples separately in Table 4, giving on the left side the percentage of all nests of known outcome, at whatever stage they were found, which were counted as successful because at least one young tanager was reared in each of them; and on the right side the number of eggs in nests found early which yielded fledglings. In our samples, nests found early were about 5 percent less successful than those found at all stages.

For the Scarlet Tanager, the only one of the six species parasitized by cowbirds, I have excluded the alien eggs and young, which contributed nothing to the reproduction of the tanagers themselves. If the cowbirds' progeny were included, the egg success of this small sample would be twice as great as indicated in the table, or 53.2 percent, thus conforming to the generalization that birds in the temperate zones nest more successfully than those in or near tropical rain forests rife with predators. Only a fraction of the young birds that leave successful nests survive the perilous fledgling stage and the somewhat less hazardous juvenile stage to attain adult competence in foraging and escaping dangers. To know the value of this fraction would be to know the true measure of reproductive success, but it is extremely difficult to learn.

Table 4. Nesting success of tanagers

	Nests found at all stages			Nests found before or at start of incubation			
Species	Total	Successful	Nest success (%)	Eggs laid	Eggs hatched	Young fledged	Egg success (%)
Silver-throated Tanager	35	19	54.3	47	28	21	44.7
Golden-masked Tanager	35	10	28.6	40	23	8	20.0
Blue-gray Tanager	42	20	47.6	50	34	22	44.0
Gray-headed Tanager	24	9	37.5	35	17	9	25.7
Scarlet-rumped Tanager	163	63	38.6	207	121	86	41.5
Scarlet Tanager	16	8	50.0	30[1]	8	8	26.6

1. Does not include eggs of the Brown-headed Cowbird.

The enemies of adult tanagers are mostly different from those that destroy their nests. In the north, Scarlet Tanagers are frequent victims of Screech Owls, one of whose nests contained remains of eight, mostly adult females. Long-eared Owls and Short-eared Owls have also been recorded as predators on tanagers, as have hawks, although apparently less frequently. Against nocturnal owls, tanagers are helpless, but when alert they may escape diurnal raptors. I have only once seen a hawk capture a tanager. As a small hawk bore away a Scarlet-rumped Tanager from the feeder toward the forest, the victim in the constricting talons cried piteously.

If they escape all enemies, tanagers may live a long while. Individuals sheltered and well attended in captivity reveal their potential longevity, which is seldom realized in hazardous freedom. A pair of tiny Red-legged Honeycreepers were still alive after twenty-four years in an aviary. A Western Tanager, picked up after a violent storm in the state of Washington, survived for fifteen years and four months in captivity. A Scarlet Tanager was still alive ten and a half years after he was brought to his guardian as a nestling with a broken wing.

In the humid tropics the average life-span of unsheltered small birds is substantially longer than it is where winter is severe and many birds therefore undertake hazardous migrations, but far fewer have been given numbered bands, which might reveal how long they survive. In Trinidad a free male Silver-beaked Tanager was nine and a half years old when recaptured, and a female was at least eight years old. A Palm Tanager was at least nine years old and a Blue-gray Tanager no less than seven years. How much longer any of these free birds lived is not known. In Panama a Blue-gray Tanager, banded as an adult, was found dead nine and a half years later. A Bay-headed Tanager in Trinidad survived for at least five years. All of these tropical tanagers were recaptured at or near the sites where they had been banded years earlier, confirming the impression that they do not wander far. The annual survival rates of populations of passerine birds, including tanagers, in the humid tropics are 80 percent or more; in contrast, the rates for adult passerines in Europe and America north of Mexico are only 30 to 50 percent.

Despite their beauty, tanagers appear to be less seriously affected by the nefarious international "pet" trade than some other birds, especially parrots. However, in the tropical countries where they are native, euphonias, who sing persistently rather than brilliantly, are too frequently trapped, confined in tiny cages, and carelessly attended—a severe penalty for being lovely and songful. But tanagers have no greater enemies than the men who, throughout tropical America, are destroying their habitats at a reckless rate or poisoning them with biocides, thereby threatening the survival of many species whose ways of life have never been studied.

12 Tanagers and Man

Tanagers seldom clash with human interests. Sometimes Summer Tanagers, in both their summer and winter homes, frequent the neighborhood of beehives and catch so many of the domestic bees—reducing the production of honey—that bee-keepers shoot them, even if reluctantly. When Western Tanagers in their spring migration pass through the major fruit-growing districts of California instead of, as more usually, the foothills of the mountain ranges, they may in some years seriously damage ripening cherries. On the other hand, Scarlet Tanagers are credited with protecting apple orchards and other trees, especially oaks, by consuming great quantities of defoliating caterpillars, wood-boring beetles, and weevils. The insects eaten by northern tanagers include many hymenopterous species regarded as beneficial because they parasitize and reduce the numbers of insects injurious to plants of economic value; however, the birds may compensate for the reduction of the parasites by directly consuming the parasites' hosts. From the economic point of view, these northern tanagers appear to be far more beneficial than harmful.

I have never heard of any serious losses attributed to the much more abundant tropical tanagers, although they are among the birds that drop seeds of parasitic mistletoes on fruit trees. My only complaint against them is that they scatter over our garden so many seeds of trees and shrubs that if we did not continually pull up most of the resulting seedlings, we would live too closely pressed by a thicket or forest. But tanagers are by no means the only birds that try to convert our garden into woodland. And when I reflect that this is only an unintended side effect of their beneficent activity of disseminating the seeds of beautiful and useful plants, I forgive them for putting us to this labor. Moreover, some of the wildlings that the birds sow in our garden are worth preserving as attractive ornamentals or sources of food for the birds. As a major element in the colorful avifauna that draws many bird-watching tourists, whose spending brings foreign currency to tropical American countries burdened with huge foreign debts, tanagers may also be of considerable economic importance.

Tanagers contribute more, actually and potentially, to the human spirit than to man's economy. Their bright colors, and more rarely their songs, are an aesthetic delight. And if, while enjoying their beauty in a thoughtful mood, we reflect on their way of life and relations with one another and with birds of different species, we find additional reasons to rejoice in them. In a living world where so much is ugly and revolting—where there is so much predatory horror, bloodshed, and violence—it is re-

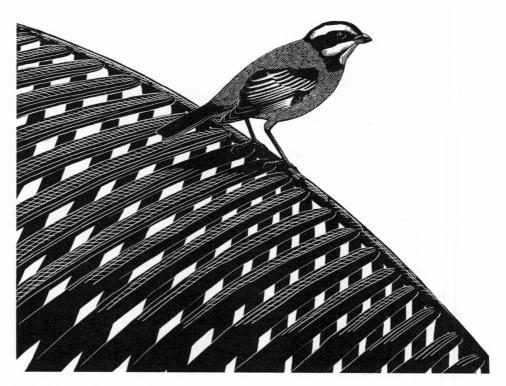

Striped-headed Tanager *Spindalis zena*
Male. Bahama Islands, Greater Antilles, Cozumel, and southern Florida.

freshing to contemplate creatures that are, on the whole, gentle and pacific, rarely quarreling among themselves, even more seldom fighting injuriously, and living in concord with birds of many other kinds which share fruiting trees with them. And when I watch the many species of tanagers that preserve close pair bonds through the long months when they are sexually quiescent, I wonder what sentiments bind them together, whether they feel anything like love or personal devotion. In many ways, tanagers are a paradigm of what some of us aspire to be.

Tanagers, like a number of other largely or wholly frugivorous birds, remind us of what the living world owes to cooperation, mutualism, and the exchange of benefits, especially between animals and the plants that support them. An immense variety of trees, shrubs, and vines not only provide abundant food for birds but attract them to it by tinting their berries and arils with colors that contrast with the verdure of foliage. Apparently, it was to help them find fruits that birds and certain mammals, including primates, developed color vision, which in turn favored the evolution of bright colors on the frugivorous animals themselves, thereby immeasurably increasing the beauty of the natural world and our delight in it. In return for nutritious fruits, birds scatter the enclosed seeds far and wide. The interactions of birds and fructiferous plants benefit both and injure neither—a pleasing contrast to innumerable other interactions between organisms of different kinds. The contemplation of tanagers and their relations with one another as well as with other birds and with plants helps us preserve a hopeful view of the potentialities of evolution—and of ourselves. It would be deplorable if, by destroying their habitats on a vast scale, we made these delightful birds rare.

Bibliography

Chapter 1 The Tanager Family
(General references, classification, anatomy, plumage, migration)

Bent, A. C. 1958. *Life Histories of North American Blackbirds, Orioles, Tanagers, and Allies.* U.S. National Museum Bulletin no. 211. (Habits and distribution of tanagers of the United States and Canada.)

Dunning, J. S. 1970. *Portraits of Tropical Birds.* Wynnewood, Pa.: Livingston Publishing Co. (Includes twenty-seven tanagers.)

Dunning, J. S. 1982. *South American Land Birds: A Photographic Aid to Identification.* Newton Square, Pa.: Harrowood Books. (Many color photographs of tanagers.)

Eisenmann, E. 1962. On the systematic position of *Rhodinocichla rosea. Auk* 79:640–648.

ffrench, R. 1973. *A Guide to the Birds of Trinidad and Tobago.* Wynnewood, Pa.: Livingston Publishing Co. (Contains much information on habits, food, and nesting.)

Haverschmidt, F. 1968. *Birds of Surinam.* Wynnewood, Pa.: Livingston Publishing Co. (Contains notes on food and breeding.)

Isler, M. L., and P. R. Isler. 1987. *The Tanagers: Natural History, Distribution, and Identification.* Washington, D.C.: Smithsonian Institution Press.

Prescott, K. W. 1965. *The Scarlet Tanager.* New Jersey State Museum Investigations no. 2. (A comprehensive study.)

Skutch, A. F. 1954. *Life Histories of Central American Birds.* Pacific Coast Avifauna no. 31. (Includes fourteen species of tanagers.)

Skutch, A. F. 1962. Life histories of honeycreepers. *Condor* 64:92–116.

Skutch, A. F. 1967. *Life Histories of Central American Highland Birds.* Nuttall Ornithological Club Publication no. 7. (Includes two species of tanagers.)

Skutch, A. F. 1972. *Studies of Tropical American Birds.* Nuttall Ornithological Club Publication no. 10. (Includes five species of tanagers.)

Skutch, A. F. 1981. *New Studies of Tropical American Birds.* Nuttall Ornithological Club Publication no. 19. (Includes five species of tanagers.)

Storer, R. W. 1969. What is a tanager? *Living Bird* 8:127–136.

Willis, E. O. 1966. Ecology and behavior of the Crested Ant-Tanager. *Condor* 68:56–71.

Chapter 2 Food and Foraging

Beehler, B. 1980. A comparison of avian foraging at flowering trees in Panama and New Guinea. *Wilson Bulletin* 92:513–519.

Hundley, M. H., and C. R. Mason. 1965. Birds develop a taste for sugar. *Wilson Bulletin* 77:408.

Skutch, A. F. 1962. On the habits of the Queo, *Rhodinocichla rosea*. *Auk* 79:633–639.

Skutch, A. F. 1980. Arils as food of tropical American birds. *Condor* 82:31–42.

Snow, B. K., and D. W. Snow. 1971. The feeding ecology of tanagers and honeycreepers in Trinidad. *Auk* 88:291–322.

Willis, E. 1960. A study of the foraging behavior of two species of ant-tanagers. *Auk* 77:150–170.

Willis, E. O. 1966. Competitive exclusion and birds at fruiting trees in western Colombia. *Auk* 83:479–480.

Winkel, W. 1969. Experimentelle Untersuchungen an Zuckervögeln (Coerebidae) im Funktionskreis der Nahrungssuche: Über die Bedeutung von Farben, Formen und Zuckerkonzentrationen. *Zeitschrift für Tierpsychologie* 26:573–608.

Chapter 3 Voice

Morton, E. S. 1976. Vocal mimicry in the Thick-billed Euphonia. *Wilson Bulletin* 88:485–486.

Remsen, J. V., Jr. 1976. Observations of vocal mimicry in the Thick-billed Euphonia. *Wilson Bulletin* 88:487–488.

Snow, B. K. 1974. Vocal mimicry in the Violaceous Euphonia, *Euphonia violacea*. *Wilson Bulletin* 86:179–180.

Willis, E. 1960. Voice, courtship, and territorial behavior of ant-tanagers in British Honduras. *Condor* 62:73–87.

Chapter 4 Daily Life

Groskin, H. 1943. Scarlet Tanagers "anting." *Auk* 60:55–59.

Skutch, A. F. 1972. (Full reference in list for chapter 1.)

Willis, E. O. 1960. Red-crowned Ant-Tanagers, Tawny-crowned Greenlets, and forest flocks. *Wilson Bulletin* 72:105–106.

Chapter 5 Displays and Disputes

Moynihan, M. 1962. Display patterns of tropical American "nine-primaried" songbirds. I. *Chlorospingus*. *Auk* 79:310–344.

Moynihan, M. 1962. Display patterns of tropical American "nine-primaried" songbirds. II. Some species of *Ramphocelus. Auk* 79:655–686.
Skutch, A. F. 1954, 1962, 1981. (Full references in list for chapter 1.)

Chapter 6   Temperament

Skutch, A. F. 1954, 1981. (Full references in list for chapter 1.)

Chapters 7, 8, and 9   Reproduction

Bent, A. C. 1958. (Full reference in list for chapter 1.)
Carvalho, C. T. de. 1957. *Notas sôbre a biologia do* Ramphocelus carbo. Boletim do Museu Paraense Emilio Goeldi no. 5, pp. 1–20.
Haverschmidt, F. 1954. Zur Brutbiologie von *Thraupis episcopus* in Surinam. *Journal für Ornithologie* 95:48–54.
Prescott, K. W. 1964. Constancy of incubation for the Scarlet Tanager. *Wilson Bulletin* 76:37–42.
Prescott, K. W. 1965. (Full reference in list for chapter 1.)
Robins, C. R., and W. B. Heed. 1951. Bird notes from La Joya de Salas, Tamaulipas. *Wilson Bulletin* 63:263–270. (Nest of Blue-hooded Euphonia.)
Russell, S. M. 1964. *A Distributional Study of the Birds of British Honduras.* American Ornithologists' Union Ornithological Monograph no. 1. (Nest of Yellow-throated Euphonia.)
Skutch, A. F. 1954, 1962, 1967, 1972, and 1981. (Full references in list for chapter 1.)
Skutch, A. F. 1968. The nesting of some Venezuelan birds. *Condor* 70:66–82. (Silver-beaked Tanager.)
Snow, D. W., and B. K. Snow. 1964. Breeding seasons and annual cycles of Trinidad land-birds. *Zoologica* (New York) 49:1–39.
Willis, E. 1961. A study of nesting ant-tanagers in British Honduras. *Condor* 63:479–503.

Chapter 10   Helpers

Hales, H. 1896. Peculiar traits of some Scarlet Tanagers. *Auk* 13:261–263. (Feeding of nestling Chipping Sparrows.)
Johnson, R. B. 1984. In letter (Thick-billed Euphonia.)
Prescott, K. W. 1965. (Full reference in list for chapter 1.)
Skutch, A. F. 1961. Helpers among birds. *Condor* 63:198–226.
Skutch, A. F. 1980. *A Naturalist on a Tropical Farm.* Berkeley: University of California Press. (Speckled Tanager.)
Skutch, A. F. 1981. (Full reference in list for chapter 1.)
Skutch, A. F. 1986. *Helpers at Birds' Nests: A World-wide Survey of Cooperative Breeding and Related Behavior.* Iowa City: University of Iowa Press.

Snow, D. W., and C. T. Collins. 1962. Social breeding behavior of the Mexican Tanager. *Condor* 64:161.

Chapter 11   Enemies, Nesting Success, and Longevity

Friedmann, H., and L. F. Kiff. 1985. The parasitic cowbirds and their hosts. *Proceedings of Western Foundation of Vertebrate Zoology* 2:226–302.

Prescott, K. W. 1947. Unusual behavior of a cowbird and Scarlet Tanager at a Red-eyed Vireo nest. *Wilson Bulletin* 59:210.

Prescott, K. W. 1965. (Full reference in list for chapter 1.)

Schumacher, D. M. 1964. Ages of some captive wild birds. *Condor* 66:309.

Skutch, A. F. 1966. A breeding bird census and nesting success in Costa Rica. *Ibis* 108:1–16.

Skutch, A. F. 1981. (Full reference in list for chapter 1.)

Snow, D. W., and A. Lill. 1974. Longevity records for some Neotropical land birds. *Condor* 76:262–267.

Terres, J. K. 1980. *The Audubon Society Encyclopedia of North American Birds.* New York: Alfred A. Knopf.

Index

All subject entries (bathing, breeding seasons, etc.) refer to tanagers. **Illustrations in boldface.**